The Secret World of the Victorian Lodging House

'With gratitude to Fiona Ashton for her sharp eye and true ear.'

The Secret World of the Victorian Lodging House

Joseph O'Neill

PEN & SWORD
HISTORY

First published in Great Britain in 2014 by
Pen & Sword History
an imprint of
Pen & Sword Books Ltd
47 Church Street
Barnsley
South Yorkshire
S70 2AS

Copyright © Joseph O'Neill 2014

ISBN 978 1 78159 393 6

A CIP catalogue record for this book is available from the British
Library

Typeset in Ehrhardt by
Mac Style, Bridlington, East Yorkshire
Printed and bound in the UK by CPI Group (UK) Ltd, Croydon,
CRO 4YY

Pen & Sword Books Ltd incorporates the imprints of Pen & Sword
Archaeology, Atlas, Aviation, Battleground, Discovery, Family History,
History, Maritime, Military, Naval, Politics, Railways, Select,
Transport, True Crime, and Fiction, Frontline Books, Leo Cooper,
Praetorian Press, Seaforth Publishing and Wharncliffe.

For a complete list of Pen & Sword titles please contact
PEN & SWORD BOOKS LIMITED
47 Church Street, Barnsley, South Yorkshire, S70 2AS, England
E-mail: enquiries@pen-and-sword.co.uk
Website: www.pen-and-sword.co.uk

Contents

Preface

I jolted awake. In an instant I was at the window. A chill moon lit the backyard. But there was no movement, nothing amiss. What had woken me? Then the gate moved on its hinges, opened a few inches, then closed with a 'chug' against the bricks. That was it – the gate banging. I crossed the room, back to the bed, my feet cold on the linoleum. Then I heard it: a clatter of aluminium.

Now there was light under my door, feet on the stairs, my mother's voice near and my father's further away. Then I was out on the stairs, my heart skittish to be up at this unknown hour, down the three flights of stairs, along the hall which was chill with the night air and running into my mother's back at the door of the kitchen. I pushed my head between her hip and the jamb of the door.

Jack lay amid the ruins of the table, its four legs like those of a stricken spider with it's back broken and about him pans and sieves, pots, jars and ladles, once housed on the shelves he had brought cascading from the wall.

The demolition of the kitchen was never broached and after a while I began to think that I had imagined the whole thing. Circumstantial evidence, however, confirmed my recollection: a new deal table appeared in the kitchen the next day. Besides, Jack was a prodigious drinker, given to concluding his evenings in the most inhospitable of places. On one occasion he was found comatose with his back resting against the door of a telephone box and on another across the bonnet of an Austin A30. The kitchen incident was akin to the evening he embraced the motoring revolution.

In the following days and weeks the lodgers continued to sit around the walls of the living room waiting for their dinner while shielded from my view by their open newspapers, as close as Roman soldiers with their shields locked together in turtle formation. They read the *Manchester Evening News*, the *Cork Weekly Examiner*, the *Irish Independent* and the *Western People*, while Radio Eireann undulated in the background. On one occasion, irked by the bookish atmosphere, I took a poker from the fire and sought to obliterate Harold Macmillan's moustache from the front page of the *Inishowen Independent*. In a flurry of flames and flapping the room filled with smoke and the entire newspaper was consigned to the hearth. My father's ire wilted in the face of the Inishowen man's indulgent laughter and some of the lodgers supported my actions, adding that 'burning is too good for that Macmillan.'

As always, they forgave me. They continued to give me half-crowns on pay day and to take me to High Mass, when occasionally during the homily my guardian would step outside to suck deep on a *Sweet Afton*. Back home, I marvelled at their big boots encrusted in ochre clay, their trousers stiff with mud, the odour of wet wool and damp earth they exuded when recently home from work and the smell of brilliantine and stale Guinness from their blue Sunday suits. Almost weekly, one of them disappeared, off to Kilburn or Digbeth, to be replaced by another from Connemara or Kilkenny.

But most of all, I wondered about why these men lived with us and not in their own homes, with their own wives and children. Who were these fourteen men my mother fed in relays each evening?

When I asked, my father said they were lodgers, men who had left home to find work. For as long as I can remember they have fascinated me. Rootless, yet of a specific time and place, they lived in a twilight place, neither at home nor settled away from home. Without the financial or social responsibilities of adults, in many ways they exemplified the ideals of working class masculinity – tough, strong and independent.

The lodging house I grew up in the 1950s was one of the last of its kind. Social and economic changes, developing patterns of migration and innovations in the building industry reduced the demand for the navvy. But the lodging house, the abode of Britain's itinerant workers, has a long and fascinating history, little of which is available to the general reader. I hope this book, the result of a long-term interest, helps to fill that gap.

Joseph O'Neill, 2014

Introduction: 'Without Seeming to Care for Each Other'

'And you did not notice, madam?' The coroner's face was puckered in an expression of outraged incredulity.

'No, sir,' replied Mary Wood, indignant at the suggestion that she was in any way blameworthy.

'The man's face was black, madam. He was in a state of decomposition', said the coroner. 'You saw him on the Wednesday and Thursday subsequent to his retiring to bed and thought nothing of it?' The coroner clearly found it impossible to imagine a situation in which a lodger could be dead in his bed for several days without his landlady noticing.

'I have known some of my lodgers,' Mary replied, ' who have been out upon the spree to lay in bed for three days together without a bit of a sup and then they have gone out to their work as well and as hearty as ever they was in their lives; I have known it often to have been done.'

The coroner shook his grey head. 'And there were seven other beds in this room?'

'Yes, sir,' Mary replied.

'And how many lodgers occupied these beds?'

'Seventeen,' she answered.

'So,' said the coroner, 'seventeen people shared a room with a putrefying corpse for three days and not one of them noticed anything amiss?'

'My lodgers comes and goes and minds their own business,' said Mary with the manner of one bestowing the highest possible accolade. 'They goes in and out without seeming to care for each other.'

The inquest into the death of 36-year-old James Parkinson, one of London's many dealers in cats' meat, in a common lodging house in West Street, Saffron Hill, in February 1834, allowed the middle classes to peep into the world of the lodging house. Their response, like that of the coroner, was appalled incredulity, with the story confirming their conviction that the common lodging house was the embodiment of evil and everything that threatened good order and human progress. The denizens of the common lodging house, it seemed, were barely human and lived in a manner that shamed a great nation.

It is impossible to peruse any local newspaper of the period without finding some mention of this ubiquitous institution and its links with crime, prostitution, drunkenness, disease, squalor, juvenile delinquency, violence and murder. To cite but one example: Jack the Ripper's victims all lived in an area in which every second house was a lodging house and at least two of the women he murdered inhabited such places.

The very term 'common lodging house', seemed to raise the hackles of the respectable. Consequently, those investigative journalists who ventured into them were sure of a rapt readership. The world their articles described was no less exotic than that of the Kalahari Bushmen and Maasai warriors; yet the lodger and the lodging house were as much features of Victorian life as the beggar and the pub. They were at the heart of every one of Britain's cities and towns and were central to working class life.

The 1851 census, for instance, shows that one in three Irishmen between 20 and 44 years of age living in England resided in lodgings. In the same year one in eight homes included a lodger of some sort. In many parts of the country, such as Nottingham and York, it was as high as one in five. There were 1,401 lodging houses listed in the London post office directory 20 years later, and this was certainly only a fraction of the true number.

Lodging houses were not new to the nineteenth century. As early as 1749 the worst part of one of London's most notorious rookeries, the streets around George Street and Church Lane, attracted the attention of Henry Fielding. The area, he said, contained 'a great number of houses set apart for the reception of rogues and vagabonds who have been lodging there for two pence a night.' He goes on to mention one woman 'who alone owns seven of these houses, all with miserable beds from cellar to garret … these beds are several in the same room, men and women, often strangers to each other lie promiscuously. Gin is sold to them at a penny a quart.'

By the mid-nineteenth century lodging houses were a feature of every city and town and formed a system of accommodation linking most parts of the country and making them accessible to travellers of small means. Most towns had a number of streets – in some cases whole districts – where several lodging houses were to be found. In the 1860s Manchester had 472 lodging houses concentrated in specific areas of the city, and 10 years later 1 in 14 people in the city's rookeries lived in one.

Yet, though they aroused widespread interest in Victorian times, there has been little written about lodging houses since. As one academic working in this area notes, 'Despite the significance of lodging in nineteenth century urban society it is rather surprising that it has received so little attention from researchers'. Speaking of the importance of the lodging house in the economy of Leicester in the nineteenth century, S.F. Page remarks on the unaccountable fact that 'it has received so little attention from researchers'. The same may be said of those who used the lodging houses. As another student of this area says, 'lodgers rarely receive sufficient attention in historical studies'.

Given the British obsession with housing, this is very curious: we imbibe details of house prices as if our entire economic well-being depends on them. Today social commentators assure us that we have a housing crisis. One recently told BBC Radio 4 that the government should put the same resources into housing as it does the NHS. These concerns are not new: Britain has been short of suitable accommodation since at least the late eighteenth century.

While our concerns about housing have remained constant, our perception of the problem has changed. Today it is a crisis if people are finding it difficult to buy their own homes. In our age of owner occupiers, in which seventy per cent of people own their own homes, it is difficult for us to grasp the prevalence of lodging in the Victorian era. As late as 1918, seventy-seven per cent of British people did not own the roof over their head – nor could they take it for granted. The majority rented or lodged. But many could not afford to pay even one week's rent in advance. Others were mobile and renting in the normal way was of no use to them even if they could afford it.

The most attractive solution for a single person was to go into a private house as a lodger – someone who provides his own food – or a boarder – one who eats with the family. In practice, the distinction between a lodger and a boarder was often blurred: many of those described as lodgers in census records were living in the home of a family member – a brother or sister, cousin, uncle or aunt – and shared family meals.

Failing that, for most of the nineteenth century there was little choice but the common lodging house, which played a significant part in working class life and in that of the underclass. Yet until now the lives of these people and their experience of the lodging house have not been discussed in a form accessible to the general reader.

Any attempt to depict the life of Victorian lodging houses must begin by placing them within the context of contemporary working class housing and tackling some of the widely accepted notions about their nature and clientele. How did these establishments compare with the other accommodation available to working people? Why were so many attracted to them, even when better accommodation was to be had at no cost? Why did they acquire such a poisonous reputation? Were all lodging houses the vile dens of thieves and tramps? Were all lodgers rogues and the people who ran the houses all professional criminals, as so many commentators believed? Why did they become such a prominent feature of working class life that hardly a centre of population anywhere in Britain did not have at least one? Were they scattered randomly or were they clustered in certain areas? What attempts were made to eliminate their undesirable features and if so, how successful were they? And finally, why did the lodging house, so prominent a feature of working class life, virtually disappear in the years immediately before the First World War?

One of the problems of discussing the common lodging house, which also bedevilled legislators, is defining exactly the sort of places with which we are concerned. The definition used for the census was a building that 'accommodates lodgers who provide themselves with food in common kitchens shared with other inmates'. The term came into widespread use in Victorian times and referred to cheap accommodation in which clients lodged in shared eating and sleeping facilities with people who were not family members. This is how it shall be used here. It shall not be used to refer to buildings used primarily as family homes in which one or a small number of non-family members also lived in common.

Fascinating as the history of the common lodging house is in its own right, it also has a wider significance: it serves as a measure of the quality of life of those who existed in that ever-shifting nether world where the poor merged with the criminal classes. It was on this opaque realm, where people defy neat categorisation and criminals rubbed shoulders with aspiring workmen, that respectable society's fears focused.

Chapter One

'Enough to Raise the Roof Off My Skull': Working Class Housing in the Nineteenth Century

In 1899 journalist Robert Blatchford went undercover in Manchester for the *Sunday Chronicle*. He walked less than half a mile from the city centre, his feet echoing through the empty streets. All the gin palaces, pubs and beerhouses had closed and the last of their patrons gone to their beds sodden with drink. The only movements were those of the cats, watching him with yellow-eyed curiosity. As he reached his destination he was conscious of a curious smell: it was the unmistakable reek of the slums, that distinctive odour of human waste and rotting rubbish. He gagged, while around his feet the cats seemed to have multiplied, a milling horde of soiled creatures, their whiskers twitching with curiosity at this outsider. Blatchford raised his head. Pushing back his shoulders, he stepped from the pavement into the narrow passageway.

Within minutes, he was lost in the 'miles of narrow, murky streets ... involuted labyrinths of courts and passages and covered ways where a devilish ingenuity shuts out light and air. Everywhere there was filth, broken pavements, ill-set roads covered with rubbish, stagnant pools of water, and dark, narrow, dilapidated, built-in hovels.'

His middle-class readers were appalled. Many refused to believe it, accusing him of exaggeration, if not blatant lies. After all, Blatchford was not reporting from darkest Africa or the bowels of a teeming oriental city. He was describing Manchester, the great industrial powerhouse which was remaking Britain, shaping the country in its own image and likeness. The horrors of which he spoke were only a few hundred yards from the city's sumptuous emporia, their plate-glass windows aglow with the light of chandeliers, displaying every luxury produced by the greatest Empire in history. Yet what Blatchford wrote was verified by other social investigators; the Reverend Bass found in Birmingham conditions as bad as those in Manchester, while others vouched that every provincial city and town had pockets of squalor to equal those of the industrial heartland.

The Industrial Revolution spawned these conditions and in so doing gave birth to a new creation: the denizen of the industrial city, slum man. The burgeoning factories that sprang up in cities and towns between 1750 and 1850 drew hordes of displaced farm labourers and destitute Irish. Many were driven to the cities, not drawn by their appeal. The rapid increase in enclosure created a new class of landless labourers with no stake in the community and little hope of employment. According to J.L and B. Hammond in the *The Village Labourer*, the small farmers of Merton, Oxfordshire, 'who had heretofore lived in comparative plenty, became suddenly reduced to the situation of labourers and in a few years had to throw themselves on the parish', or move to the towns in search of employment, were typical of millions in rural England.

The renowned commentator William Cobbett records the result of this. Writing in 1834, he was horrified by the appearance of women labourers in Hampshire – 'such an assemblage of rags as I never saw before' – and the condition of labourers near Cricklade, 'their dwellings little better than pig-beds, their food not nearly equal to that of a pig'. Relentless poverty in Ireland guaranteed a constant flow of Irish immigrants, while the end of the Napoleonic Wars in 1815 pitched thousands of soldiers onto the labour market at a time when improvements in roads and canals made it easier than ever for people to travel in search of work.

For many of the faceless throng, reaching the city was itself a feat of courage. One such was Mary Reynolds. Her husband was one of the million victims of Ireland's Great Famine. As soon as she had buried him she set out from Mohill, County Leitrim, with her six children and walked to Dublin. With her last few coppers she paid the fare to

Liverpool and having arrived in England destitute, trudged the thirty miles to Manchester.

Villages grew into great sprawling towns. In the ten years after 1821, Manchester's population increased by fifty per cent, Bradford's by eighty per cent and Birmingham, Leeds, Blackburn, Sheffield and Bolton all doubled in size in twenty years. For these newcomers the city was more than a new location; it was a remorseless engine of change more powerful than any war, invasion, revolution or disaster. It yanked the newcomers up from their roots, cut them off from their culture and traditions and shattered the pattern of lives for so long tied to the seasons and nature's rhythm. Britain was no longer a rural society in which most people lived and worked in the countryside.

It is difficult for us to grasp the speed of this change; in 1801 seventy per cent of Britain's population lived in the countryside while fifty years later it was just over fifty per cent and the balance continued to shift. In addition there was a massive influx of migrants, particularly from Ireland after 1847, most of whom sought work in the cities and towns.

The effect of this was also to change the nature of the towns: neither mid-nineteenth century Manchester nor any growing industrial centre was merely a bigger version of what it had been in 1801. This is most evident in London; by 1851 each acre of Hampstead was home to an average of less than 6 people, whereas 220 crowded together per acre in St Giles. At the same time there were 3,000 families in St Giles, each living in a single room. In Holborn, of a population of 44,000, over 12,000 lived in single rooms. This was largely because until the beginning of the twentieth century it was essential for working people to live within walking distance of their work. As late as 1880, forty per cent of those who lived in Westminster were costermongers, hawkers or cleaners who worked near their homes.

The inevitable consequence of the flight to the cities was a chronic shortage of housing. What constitutes acceptable housing varies from one period to another. Thus, in the early nineteenth century for shelter to qualify as decent accommodation all that was necessary was that it was dry, floored and included access to a reliable outside source of water. As the nineteenth century progressed, expectations increased and by the mid-century it was reasonable to expect accommodation to be sufficiently spacious to include a separate sleeping area for adult offspring and parents, in addition to adequate drainage and a safe reliable water supply. It was not until the twentieth century that people might expect an indoor lavatory. By that time it was also reasonable to expect a dwelling such that any competent woman might keep it clean and free of vermin.

In the nineteenth century, as now, one man's needs are another man's business opportunity and with this acute overcrowding came attractive prospects for the speculative builder. The cheapest land was near to the factories and mills, which was ideal for development as workers' housing. It was there, in the valley of the River Don in Sheffield, near the Rea and Hockley Brook in Birmingham and even in smaller industrial areas, such as between the Abbey and the Avon in Bath, that the working class areas grew up. They were prone to flooding, the effects of poor drainage, and perpetual dampness.

The builders' aim was to maximise profit. Houses were built back-to-back and often so close together that in areas of Nottingham the space between one row of front doors and another was literally an arm's length. Without building regulations, planning procedures, sanitary inspections or even accepted standards of workmanship, the result was jerry-building of the shoddiest kind. The 1842 Royal Commission on Housing found that these houses:

> are often built of the commonest materials, and with the worst workmanship, and are altogether unfit for the people to live in. The old houses are rotten from age and neglect. The new often commence where the old leave off and are rotten from the first. It is quite certain that the working classes are largely housed in dwellings many of which would be unsuitable even if they were not overcrowded.

Before long, the builders were resorting to 'in-filling' – squeezing a row of houses into the back gardens of existing houses. In districts once occupied by the middle classes the large houses they left in their flight to the suburbs were ideal for multiple occupancy and their enormous gardens were soon filled with courts. This was a feature of Manchester's Angel Meadow slum, which so appalled Marx and Engels and contributed significantly to their belief that capitalism was an inherently dehumanising system. In such places there was seldom a safe water supply, with the result that in areas like Hyde the poor paid a shilling a week to water carriers. The sight of children begging for water was common and there were frequent reports of water being stolen.

The builders' liking for arranging houses into courts – four rows of houses looking in on a communal area – made conditions worse. In the dock area of Hull, the interconnecting courts had only one entrance from the road. The scourge of the Glasgow poor, however, was not the claustrophobic court but the seething tenement, generally accepted as the worst housing of the day. When Edwin Chadwick, the great sanitary reformer, visited the city, he found, 'There were no privies or drains… and the dungheaps received all filth which the swarm of wretched inhabitants could give.'

All this must be viewed within the context of the industrial workers' economic situation, which was generally one of abject poverty. In good times, when they were young and healthy, they could feed themselves, keep a roof over their heads and afford essential clothing. The slightest deviation from these ideal circumstances plunged them into destitution and the precariousness of their meagre existence undermined any sense of security. They existed on the lip of the abyss, disaster an ever-present threat, unable to take anything for granted. Economic downturns plunged millions into want.

It was a Manchester man, Dr James Kay, who more than any single person brought the horrors of slum life before the British public and, through his influence on Engels, to the attention of the world. His description of the housing of the Manchester cotton workers in *The*

Moral and Physical Condition of the Working Class Employed in the Cotton Manufacture in Manchester, published in 1832, made Manchester synonymous with all the evils of the new age. He told of a one-room cellar, home to sixteen people and a host of animals. He described rooms so small that it was impossible to stand upright, the ceilings black with cockroaches and every inch of the floor covered with bodies huddled on fetid straw. He found hordes of people living without water, ventilation, sanitation or adequate natural light.

When Engels was researching *The Condition of the Working Class in England* twelve years later, things were little better. Referring to Angel Meadow, he wrote:

> Four thousand human beings, most of them Irish, live there. The cottages are dirty and of the meanest sort, the streets uneven, in parts without drains or pavements; masses of refuse, offal and sickening filth lie among the standing pools in all directions; the atmosphere is poisoned by the effluvia from these and darkened by the smoke of a dozen tall chimneys. A horde of ragged women and children swarm about here, as filthy as the swine that thrive upon the garbage heaps and in the puddles.

Parts of Salford he found were just as bad: 'In this district I found a man, apparently sixty years old, living in a cow stable.'

Wherever he delved in the great cities, the social explorer found the same horrors. Their accounts are interchangeable. But few expressed the reality of squalor more powerfully than the tenant talking of the court he inhabited in Leeds. 'It is inundated with filth,' he said, 'having a most intolerable stench proceeding from two ash-pits in the adjoining courts having oozed through the wall.' The stench, he said, 'is enough to raise the roof off my skull.'

Of all the grim abodes that fascinated middle class readers none exercised lurid appeal like the cellars. Most consisted of one small room, rented at about 1*s* to 1*s* 6*d* a week in the 1850s, at a time when a labourer earned about

12*s* a week. Usually, as described by Dr James Kay, 'it is kitchen, living room, bedroom – all in one.' Dr Kay first brought the cellars to public attention in 1832. Evidence of their enduring interest emerged in 2010 when Oxford Archaeology North excavated some of the cellars in Manchester's Angel Meadow. The archaeologists are, however, only the most recent in the long line of those to study these subterranean dwellings.

In 1849 a Scots journalist, Angus Bethune Reach, reported on the area for the *Morning Chronicle*. The population density of Angel Meadow was then in excess of 350 per acre, or four times that of the city today and had already attracted the attention in 1836 of Elizabeth Gaskell, who described the cellars as the 'the very picture of loathsomeness' and 'receptacles of every species of vermin which can infest the human body'. More dispassionately, the *Builder* in 1844 labelled them 'dark, damp, ill-ventilated and dirty'.

Visiting a cellar that was home to Irish immigrants, Reach noted that the room measured only 12ft by 8ft and that the ceiling was so low that all the occupants permanently stooped. In a corner, a dozen famished figures huddled round a fire. The family made matches and the splinters of wood were piled in a corner where two children used them for their bed. He was told that another twelve people also lived in the cellar. In the 1830s, 18,000 people lived in Manchester cellars, a third of them Irish. By 1851 this figure had reached 45,000 and 50,000 in Liverpool.

The worst cellars of all were in closed courts or under back-to-back houses. Many were only a single room, between 6ft and 9ft square. They had no lighting, water or sanitation. Many of the streets had no drainage or sewerage and were often subject to seepage from the sewers. Sometimes the floor was flagged but often it consisted of nothing but bare earth.

Generally the rent for a cellar was half that of accommodation in the house above. Many of the Irish cellar dwellers were employed in the worst paid jobs and could afford nothing else. Apart from the many casual labourers, others worked as hawkers and street vendors. Large numbers laboured as porters in Manchester's Smithfield Market or as dealers in second-hand clothes, though some also worked in the cotton mills.

If conditions in the towns were frightful, the countryside was little better. Much as the Victorians loved to contrast urban squalor with an earlier rural idyll, the reality was different. In fact, many historians now argue that the new urban dwellers, drawn to the burgeoning cities by the prospect of employment, were prepared to live in squalor partly because they knew nothing better. Some market towns, like Shrewsbury, were subjected to a public health inquiry in 1854 because death rates were so high. The findings showed that the average labourer's cottage suffered from rising damp, vermin-infested wattle and daub and a leaky thatched roof.

The rural population had also boomed at the dawn of the nineteenth century – just as the number of cottages decreased. The 1843 Report on the Employment of Women and Children in Agriculture recounts twenty-nine people under one roof, eleven adults in one small bedroom, holes in roofs, and women giving birth on the floor.

When the displaced farm labourer arrived in the city in search of work he joined the scramble for shelter. His first port of call was likely to be a common lodging house. These came in a variety of forms and had a range of names. The bad ones were known as 'doss houses', 'flop houses', 'netherskens' and 'paddingkens'. In many such places residents slept on the floor, in passageways and crammed so closely up against others that anyone attempting to enter the room was obliged to step on prostrate bodies. Common lodging houses favoured by criminals were known as 'flash houses', a term also applied to public houses, coffee shops and cook shops where thieves and prostitutes hung out.

Just as lodging houses varied greatly, there were also marked regional differences in the quality of housing. For instance, there were far more cellar dwellers in the north of England than elsewhere and they were concentrated in Manchester, Liverpool and Salford. In the early 1840s, ten per cent of Liverpool's population lived in cellars. They became so closely linked in the public mind to cholera and typhus that most were closed by the local authorities in the 1870s.

It is difficult to exaggerate the effect of infectious diseases on middle-class attitudes to the slums and lodging houses in particular. Housing suddenly became a matter of life and death; infectious diseases were no respecters of class but killed indiscriminately. Typhoid even claimed Prince Albert, Queen Victoria's consort.

Before cholera arrived on these shores, Britain suffered a long and dreadful period of anticipation. As early as 1818 stories abounded of a fearful plague that drove terror-stricken inhabitants before it and, in a single day, slaughtered 500 of the British garrison in India. As it crept inexorably towards Britain, its ferocity increased. In Teheran and Basra it massacred 15,000 inhabitants in a fortnight. In a single day it claimed 30,000 Egyptian victims.

When cholera hit Europe its effects became, according to educated opinion, even more dangerous in that it undermined the social order as slum dwellers claimed that it was deliberately spread by the wealthy to cull the poor. Mobs stormed the homes of the Hungarian nobility and butchered entire families, and when the troops were called out they mutinied and murdered their officers. In Russia, where it took a particularly heavy toll, hordes stormed the hospitals and slaughtered doctors and nurses. According to *The Times*, 'no rank escapes its attack ... whole families are exterminated: civilised nations turn to savage hordes ... all grades and bonds of social organisation disappear.'

By the summer of 1831 nearly every European capital and all the Baltic ports and Hamburg, with which Britain had daily contact, were afflicted. While the disease was raging in Riga there were almost 800 ships in the city's harbour waiting to sail to Britain. The *Methodist Magazine* described what happened when the plague struck these ports: 'To see a number of our fellow creatures, in good health and in the midst of their years, suddenly seized by the most violent spasms and in a few hours cast into the tomb, is calculated to shake the firmest nerves and inspire dread in the stoutest heart.' The writer was not exaggerating: between forty and sixty per cent of those affected died, many within hours. Yet they were more fortunate than those who expired after suffering several days of violent stomach pains, vomiting, diarrhoea and total prostration.

The omens in the summer of 1831 were of biblical proportions. In the north east of England sheep suffered badly from liver disease, the rot, and there was a plague of horseflies. The air was full of moths and bumble bees. In Durham an immense swarm of green toads appeared. The imperceptible pulse of the cholera sufferer led to stories of patients being buried alive and there were chilling tales of a woman on an autopsy table pleading for her life as medical students stood poised over her with gleaming scalpels.

Sure enough, the first victim was in the north east in 1831. When he fell ill his family feared the worst and soon his blackened flesh confirmed it. In a few hours he aged 20 years; he acquired the face of a mummified corpse, demented eyes staring out from deep sockets. Like a strip of dead flesh, his tongue flopped from his mouth. His pulse was feeble. Gnawing cramps and violent vomiting and purging racked his body. But it was the colour of his black flesh, cold and damp to the touch, that left no doubt.

William Sproat, a keelman of Fish Quay, Sunderland was the first official casualty. The fearful waiting was over. Cholera had arrived in Britain. In the 35 years following 1831 there were 4 major outbreaks: 1831–2 when 32,000 died; 1848–9, 62,000; 1853–4 when it killed 20,000; and finally in 1866–7 when it claimed 14,000 lives. In an age when tuberculosis, diphtheria, enteric fever and smallpox regularly scythed great swathes through the population, cholera's death toll was relatively small. But its impact was profound. What added to the terror it evoked was the helplessness of the medical profession: there was no agreed prevention or cure. In the words of the *Lancet*, 'every doctor in the country has his own theory and no two agree.'

Gateshead, the next town to suffer after Sunderland, was typical of the areas in which cholera thrived. Its population of miners, factory workers, fishermen, ship-owners and lodging housekeepers was a cross-section of English society. Conditions were also typical. In Ropery Bank, there were a hundred families without a privy between them. In North Shields there were 7,000 people with access to only 32 lavatories, mainly in the homes of tradesmen. As late as 1849 only 300 of the 4,000 houses had piped water. It was among the poor living in such conditions that death rates were highest. The press used the terms 'fever dens' and 'slums' interchangeably.

The disease struck Gateshead with terrifying speed: over Christmas night 1831, fifty-five people were seized and thirty-two died before dusk on Boxing Day. One doctor wrote, 'the panic of the inhabitants was greater than I ever witnessed under any pestilence'. *The Times* described it as 'the most terrific attack ... in Europe. In the space of 45 hours 119 people were seized and 52 had died.' It spread rapidly to surrounding villages. In Newburn, five miles from Newcastle, half the population was affected. A few days earlier it struck across the border.

Just before Christmas cholera was reported in Haddington in East Lothian. From there it spread to Edinburgh and Glasgow and then the Highlands and the North. Fear of infection led to bizarre practices. In Musselburgh, those who died were buried in a pit 30ft deep and the bodies and bedclothes of victims sprinkled with vinegar. Yet the disease claimed 250 victims within five weeks and fear of potential carriers turned into paranoia.

At Broxbourne a sick traveller was driven out to die on the roadside. A woman who fell ill dragged herself to her mother's house. The locals heard of it, drove her away and the next day forced out her mother and burnt her home and belongings. The woman died fifteen hours later and the villagers were so terrified that none would help at her funeral. The undertaker left the coffin by the road for the doctors to deposit the corpse, used a hired horse and interred the body outside the village churchyard.

In many small fishing villages like Collieston there developed a communal neurosis. People shunned each other for fear of contagion. But worst affected of all was Edinburgh, where the local Board of Health, assisted by the city's eminent medical fraternity, had made meticulous preparations. Despite this there were 2,000 cases and half died.

Glasgow raised a massive public subscription to finance measures against the outbreak and even closed theatres and churches. Yet cholera ran rampant through the slums, and in one week there were 800 cases and 350 deaths. It was the worst affected city outside London and four out of five nurses in the city hospital died.

Many once thriving centres were turned into ghost towns, their shops closed and their streets empty. Near Cromarty the dead were left unburied for fear of touching the corpses. People fled from the towns and lived in caves.

In this first outbreak about 10,000 Scots lost their lives. One great concern was that even the esteemed Scottish medical fraternity was totally at a loss as to how to deal with the disease. But there was one thing that was indisputable: the disease flourished in poverty and filth.

When it struck London the disease hit the people of Rotherhithe and Limehouse hardest, as they, according to one doctor, were in 'the most abject state of poverty without beds to lie upon. The men live by casual labour and often get no more than four or five hours employment a week.' Within the month there were over 500 deaths.

Leeds enjoyed the dubious reputation of being the filthiest city in England and cholera claimed 700 lives there. In Liverpool 1,500 died but this figure does not include those who sailed out of Liverpool. Optimistic about the prospect of life in the New World, many ended up wrapped in sailcloth, their corpses bobbing in the vessel's wake.

The worst areas in Manchester were deemed so bad that many experts were convinced that the disease would destroy the entire working population of the city. These predictions proved overly pessimistic, though certain areas were decimated. Accounts of the progress of the disease in the city tell of characters who might have stepped off the pages of a Dickens novel.

In the garret of a lodging house in Blakely Street, one of Manchester's most infamous thoroughfares, twenty boarders shared seven beds. The first victims were the wife of a black man, who performed at country fairs as a juggler, and 'Long Jim', a dissolute drunk, famous for the expertness with which he swallowed a sword a yard long. The next day 'an inveterate old sot', Jane Robinson, fell ill and the following morning a deformed little man called 'Sailor Jack', who went on crutches and who had lost his jacket in a drunken street riot the night before, began suddenly to complain of illness. Both were soon dead. The surviving lodgers fled in terror. One walked the eighteen miles to Warrington carrying a babe in arms. When she arrived in the market place she collapsed. Those who came to her aid found that the child clutched to her breast was dead.

Yet, of all the towns affected Bilston in the West Midlands inexplicably suffered most. All the medical authorities agreed that the town, built on high, well-drained ground, was exceptionally healthy. Yet one in six of the population contracted the disease and the epidemic created 150 cholera widows and 400 cholera orphans.

Cholera's second visitation claimed even more victims than the other three. The disease was probably carried by sailors from Hamburg, one of the worst affected European cities. The towns blighted in the first wave were again stricken and in many instances it returned to the same streets and houses. In December 1848 it swept away 180 children in Tooting Poorhouse.

The third wave in 1853 is chiefly remembered because it brought a 33-year-old nurse to the attention of the British public. Florence Nightingale was in charge of cholera patients at the Middlesex Hospital. The great forbidding building catered for the East End's slum dwellers. Swamped by an unmanageable number of patients, Florence did not allow her familiarity with suffering to dull her compassion. Some victims she remembered in particular: 'The prostitutes came in perpetually, poor creatures, staggering off their beat: it took worse hold on them than on any. One poor girl, loathsomely filthy, came in and was dead in four hours. I held her in my arms and heard her saying: "Pray God that you may never be in the despair as I am in at this time".'

Not long after, the British army in the Crimea was laid to waste by an outbreak of cholera. Some regiments lost 77 per cent of their strength and in total 30,000 died. Florence Nightingale's efforts on behalf of the troops made her known throughout the world.

The final major outbreak of the century is associated with another Victorian hero. At the height of the epidemic a young man who was planning to travel to China as a medical missionary, arrived at the London Hospital. Thomas Barnardo's experience of visiting the homes of the poor led him to found a boys' home in Stepney, the forerunner of Dr Barnardo's Homes. By the end of his life he had helped 250,000 children.

For some commentators, the public disorder that attended the disease was one of its most alarming effects. *The Times* spoke of cities thrown into 'complete panic' and in 1832 cholera riots occurred in London, Manchester, Exeter, Birmingham, Bristol, Leeds, Sheffield, Glasgow, Edinburgh, Greenwick, Cathcart, Paisley and Dumfries.

The worst of these was in Manchester, where the unfortunate Mrs Butler and her two daughters were forced into the Knott Mill Hospital and locked in at night. The following morning all three were dead. Gruesome tales about the cause of their demise began to circulate and two weeks later a mob of several thousand filled the streets around the hospital. Those at the front were carrying a tiny casket containing a child who had died in the hospital. The parents had received the body in a sealed coffin and buried it without opening it. After the funeral, stories of the doctors murdering and dismembering patients began to circulate. The body was exhumed. The child was found to be headless.

The irate mob broke into the hospital, released the patients and destroyed the furniture. Both the police and the military were required to restore order. The Manchester poor blamed doctors for the spread of the disease. Many of the other contemporary theories now sound equally implausible, but a large body of medical opinion was convinced that conditions in the cities promoted the disease. The epidemic stimulated interest in the realities of working class life, something of which the majority of the middle classes were totally ignorant.

In turn, these revelations of the appalling living conditions of the poor spurred the sanitary movement of the 1840s, led by Edwin Chadwick. He believed in the need for hygienic housing, paved roads, piped water and efficient sewers. His campaigns and the fear of cholera were major factors behind the Public Health Bill, 1848, and legislation such as the Artisans' Dwelling Act, which did so much to destroy the disease's breeding grounds. But it was only in 1883 that the actual cholera microbe, the *comma bacillus*, was identified by a German doctor, Robert Koch, confirming the findings of Dr John Snow, who in 1849 put forward the theory that it was carried in water.

The immediate effect of the cholera outbreaks – the closure of many cellars – led to people crowding into the back-to-back houses built in courtyards – the next rung up the housing ladder. The back-to-back is constructed so that the back of one house is joined to the back of another and it shares two side walls with the adjacent houses. This was the dominant form of housing for the poor in the West Midlands, West Yorkshire and south-east Lancashire. Until the 1840s it represented seventy per cent of the total housing stock in Liverpool, Leeds, Nottingham, Birmingham, Keighley and Huddersfield. The last back-to-back survived in Birmingham until the end of the 1960s.

Each row faced a courtyard with communal facilities – lavatories, wash-houses and 'miskins', where the rubbish was dumped. Most houses occupied a piece of land no more than 15ft square (5ft by 3ft). Cooking was at first on an open fire and later on a range. Often the flooring was of quarry tiles covered with a 'peg rug' – hessian sacking onto which women stitched old rags. Some had three storeys, with one room on each level. Rent was about 3s 6d a week in the mid-nineteenth century, or about a fifth of a labourer's weekly wage.

Next came the 'two-up, two-down'. These were also terraced houses but were 'through-houses', i.e. unattached to another house at the rear, with a front and a rear entrance. They were found everywhere – as common in the poorest parts of Manchester and Salford as in Northampton. The mortar between the bricks was a breeding ground for little brown bugs, 'plaster beetles', which were a constant menace to householders as they often infested food and fabrics. Floored with flag stones, the walls were whitewashed.

The typical living room was about 10ft square, with a fireplace in a chimney breast, an oven and a table. There was a tiny back kitchen, typically with a small table, a boiler and wall shelves. Coal was kept under the staircase. The bigger bedroom could barely accommodate two double beds and the smaller was only big enough for a single. It was not uncommon for families of twelve to live in such houses.

The position of the tenement in the housing hierarchy is ambiguous. Multiple-occupancy buildings were of two types – the purpose-built and those that started out as prestigious residences before being split up into living quarters for numerous families and then declining into slums. The former was common in the industrial areas of Scotland and was home to respectable working men, such as skilled craftsmen and engineers, as well as the poor.

Tenements in England tended to be large houses modified for multiple occupancy by a landlord who furnished them for a few shillings. The All Saints area in Newcastle in the 1850s was a good example. But the most infamous 'rookeries' were in London, at St Giles, Saffron Hill, Seven Dials and Jacob's Island in Bermondsey. As late as 1900, conditions in London tenements were appalling. The rent for a room at the top of a Bethnal Green tenement, entered through a trapdoor, was 2*s* 6*d* a week – half what was paid by those living immediately below in two rooms. Water was carried from a tap in the small, communal back garden where the privy was located.

As the nineteenth century progressed, conditions improved. The 1844 Royal Commission on housing found that 'though there was a great improvement in the condition of the houses of the poor as compared to thirty years ago, yet the evils of overcrowding, especially in London, were still a public scandal and were in certain areas more serious than they ever were'. The worst overcrowding was often found in small towns, where chronic shortage of housing was at its most acute. In the 1880s the Royal Commission on the Housing of the Working Classes found the worst examples in the smaller centres of population, such as Camborne in Cornwall and Alnwick in the north east.

The data on overcrowding in the industrial towns makes dismal reading. A survey of 800 Bury families in 1842 showed that in 200 cases 3 slept to a bed, and 4 to a bed in 61. In Bristol ten per cent of families occupied only part of a room and almost forty per cent rented a single room. Only twenty-five per cent enjoyed the luxury of two rooms. Similar results were found in the East End at the same time. But worst of all was the overcrowding in Liverpool. In one street the average number of people per room was over thirteen.

In this respect too, things improved after 1850. The situation in Glasgow demonstrates this. Whereas in 1871, thirty per cent of the city's population occupied only one room, by 1891 the figure was down to eighteen per cent. It is also important to remember that conditions varied greatly both between and within different parts of the country. Even in Manchester the skilled workman might live in a house with a cellar, two living rooms, two bedrooms and a small garden. In Nottingham, lace-makers lived in far better conditions than the impoverished frame-makers. Similarly, in Kentish Town, London the skilled engineers lived in housing often indistinguishable from that of the lower middle class.

As early as 1840 enlightened towns appointed an Improvement Commissioner and a strong landlord might also exercise a beneficial effect. Engels cites the case of Ashton under Lyne, where the Earl of Stamford held sway: 'The streets are broader and cleaner, while the new, bright-red cottages give every appearance of comfort.' Then there were the philanthropists who pioneered improved housing and provided the best workers' homes in the world. Their work preceded the improvements achieved by legislation and public authorities and set new standards and higher expectations.

The most feted of these is Robert Owen. Yet Owen didn't establish the famous model village at New Lanark. The cotton manufactory founded in 1784 on the Falls of Clyde was the work of David Dale, Glasgow banker and manufacturer. His initial work force of 500 children came from the Edinburgh workhouse and was accommodated in a large, new, purpose-built house. To attract adult workers he built low-rent houses. By the end of the century he had 4 mills and over 1,300 employees, whose living conditions were excellent.

Owen bought the mills in 1793 and introduced a grocery shop, vegetable market, school, bakery and wash-house for his employees. He improved the existing houses and built new ones to higher specifications with larger rooms, good windows and solid walls. Children between five and ten years old were put into full-time education. Fellow industrialists regarded Owen as a misguided eccentric, yet he confounded his critics by increasing profits from a flourishing enterprise.

Such is Owen's stature as a model employer that he has cast a shadow of obscurity over other philanthropists. In reality there are many who also deserve to be remembered, if only because they provided workers with housing so much better than the contemporary norm. Colonel Edward Akroyd, MP for Halifax, is one of these early improvers. His first model village was Copley, built between 1844 and 1853, two miles south of Halifax.

Akroyd had a keen appreciation of the natural and man-made environment and was anxious to protect it from violence. His workers' houses were back-to-back but 'built in a modified Old English style, approximating to the character of the old dwellings in the neighbourhood.' In front of the cottages, facing a river, were allotments, flanked by a recreation ground, a neo-Gothic church, a school and playgrounds. A classroom served as the village library and newsroom.

His second venture was far more ambitious. Stung by criticism of his back-to-back houses, Akroyd was determined that Akroydon, near the centre of Halifax, should be beyond reproach. He commissioned the eminent Victorian architect George Gilbert Scott. Work on the two-storey houses, built in what Akroyd described as 'domestic Gothic', began in 1861. The stone and slate cottages overlooked a green. Initially comprising a living room, a scullery or wash kitchen, a main bedroom and children's bedroom, later versions were even more spacious with a parlour and third bedroom. In an age when virtually all workers' accommodation was rented, Akroyd took the revolutionary step of setting up a home-ownership scheme.

Until recently, Sir Titus Salt was forgotten outside his locality. Then Bill Bryson, the best-selling travel writer, chanced upon Saltaire, north of Bradford, and restored interest in the alpaca-fabric manufacturer. Between 1850 and 1863 Salt created a living complex more spectacular than anything else in the country. His factory, built in the style of the Italian Renaissance, was the length of St Paul's Cathedral and the whole settlement was designed to be self-sufficient. The workers' cottages, with a living room, scullery and two to four bedrooms, were models of their kind. Water and gas were supplied and each had a private yard with a privy, coal store and ashpit. At his own expense he provided a school, hospital, chapels, reading rooms, public baths and a gym with Turkish baths.

Lord Lever's creation at Port Sunlight near Liverpool, built in 1888, also caught Bryson's eye during his tour of Britain. It incorporates a diversity of styles with houses either semi-detached or built in groups of four to six, separated by open spaces. George Cadbury, who built Bournville in 1879, also believed in the importance of space. By 1912 he had built 1,000 houses, none of which took up more than a quarter of its building plot.

From 1886 companies were encouraged to borrow at reduced rates from the Public Works Loans Commissioners to build workers' houses. Philanthropists such as the American merchant George Peabody provided multi-storey blocks of one- to three-bedroom flats, usually with shared sinks and WCs. By 1887 the Peabody Trust had provided 5,000 dwellings and greatly improved living conditions in the centre of London.

At the beginning of the twentieth century enlightened local authorities, such as Newcastle upon Tyne, began to provide houses that were 'judiciously planned ... of four rooms each, well adapted for families of a certain rank whose convenience is seldom consulted by building speculators', as described by Eneas Mackenzie in 'The present state of Newcastle: Streets within the walls', in his *Historical Account of Newcastle-upon-Tyne: Including the Borough of Gateshead*. But despite all these great improvements, it was not the philanthropist who shaped the housing of the majority of working people. The quality of their accommodation remained subject to the vagaries of the market and the conditions they endured were the result of a chronic shortage of affordable accommodation for those at the bottom of the economic pile. For many of these people the prospect of even a rented room was beyond their wildest expectations. The choice they faced was stark: 'the spike' (tramp ward of the poorhouse) or a bed shared with a stranger.

Chapter Two

'A Stain of Blood Bigger than a Man's Hand': Aversion to the Poorhouse and the Draw of the Fire

When James Greenwood first stood in line outside the tramp ward of the poorhouse he discovered something he had never suspected. Those hunched in the savage cold queuing for one of the scarce beds were entertained by an orchestra like none he had ever heard.

Every instrument was a human body and the sounds all coughs. 'Every variety of cough that I ever heard was to be heard there,' he said. It was a concerto of coughs with 'the hollow cough; the short cough; the hysterical cough; the bark that comes at regular intervals, like the quarter chiming of a clock, as to mark off the progress of decay'. The instruments were both great and small, 'with coughs from vast hollow chests and coughing from little narrow ones', all perfectly timed, 'now one, now another, now two or three together', while suspense was maintained by the intermittent gaps as there was also 'a minute's interval of silence in which to think of it all, and wonder who would begin next'.

The experience got no better when the doors opened and Greenwood and the other fortunate ones were counted by the beefy hand of the Tramp Major, who then turned away the rest into the snarl of the wind and the hailstones that began to ping off the sandstone walls of the poorhouse. Each man passing through the door raised his arms like a wounded crow attempting flight while the porter searched him. Once through the door Greenwood's breath plumed in front of him: it was as if the great stones of the stark room, reeking of astringent antiseptic, exuded a chill.

'Strip! Get them rags folded nice and neat in front of you!' said the Major, pointing with a length of three by two timber to the ground in front of their feet. The men piled their clothes before them and shuffled, white and vulnerable as shell-less snails, into a line before three enormous lead hip baths.

'Jump in!' said the Major, waving the length of timber towards the three great lead baths. The men lowered themselves into the water, wincing as the cold gripped their limbs and knotted their wasted calves and thighs. The porter handed the men in the baths a lump of carbolic soap. Immediately they set to rubbing their heads feverishly with the soap as if by the vigour of their efforts they might coax some warmth into their quivering limbs. Instantly, the water turned the colour of a pigeon's chest.

Greenwood did a mental calculation: he would get to the bath after seven other men had used it.

That night in his cell, clad in his institutional nightshirt, as he was about to lie down he saw 'in the middle of his mattress, a stain of blood bigger than a man's hand'. Once under his single blanket he couldn't control his shivering. He felt that he might well vomit the bread, vegetable gruel and water he had eaten for his supper. The reek of the carbolic soap filled the room.

The following morning he was woken by a silent porter and locked in a cell opposite the one he had slept in. The limewashed walls were blank, except for a metal grille at the base of the outside wall. A pile of rocks, a sledge hammer and a shovel rested against another wall. He knew that when he had broken the rocks into stones small enough to shovel through the grill he would get his breakfast of bread, gruel and water.

After Greenwood had eaten the porter returned his clothes – crumpled and reeking of rotten egg after fumigation. He walked out into the bright morning and realised that no amount of washing or burning of clothes would rid him of the smell of that place. In fact, it took many years for the aura of the workhouse to dissipate. Decades after the last one closed, the fear and stigma associated with it still resonated. As late as the 1960s older people rhetorically referred to the workhouse as shorthand for humiliating penury and shameful destitution. To enter the workhouse was to abandon all pretence of respectability and to admit abject failure. For itinerants there was the casual ward, or the tramp ward, the occupants of which were looked down on even by other paupers living in the main body of the workhouse.

This attitude was universal: tramps, beggars and petty thieves also looked down on those who went 'on the parish', one famously dismissing them as 'too idle to beg'. With our overweening sense of entitlement, constantly nurtured by an ubiquitous welfare apparatus that intrudes into every facet of our economic and social life, we assume the state is obliged to cosset us through every stage of our lives and cushion every inconvenience that afflicts us. Our nineteenth-century ancestors, however, valued their independence and their ability to provide for themselves. Failure to do so was shameful, proof of personal inadequacy that involved a calamitous loss of self-respect and social status.

James Greenwood's experience confirms the opinion of every other commentator on the life of the underclass: it is difficult to exaggerate their aversion to the workhouse. Many preferred not only to sleep rough but even to contrive their own imprisonment. The Manchester poor of the nineteenth century were typical: though facilities in few lodging houses equalled those of the tramp wards there, many who could not afford a lodging house slept on the brick-fields that littered the outskirts of the city. Citing figures for 1909, Mary Higgs confirms this, maintaining that 'only a small proportion of the homeless take refuge in the casual wards.'

The casual ward regime was intended to discourage the feckless, the idle and all those happy to live at the expense of rate-payers. To the Victorians, who were extravagantly charitable by modern standards, it was axiomatic that not all the poor were deserving of charity. Some were impoverished by drink, idleness, improvidence or other character defects and the notion that such people should benefit from indiscriminate charity seemed perverse morally and reprehensible: to bestow charity on the undeserving simply encourages and rewards those defects responsible, for their poverty, while also imposing an unwarranted burden on the public purse. Besides, there were other reasons not to encourage such behaviour.

The unattached, rootless and indigent wanderer has always aroused suspicion and fear. As Bob Dylan put it, 'When you ain't got nothing, you've got nothing to lose': no one is more dangerous than he who is immune to sanction. Laws restricting itinerants first appeared in the seventh century and subsequently termed them 'vagrants', 'tramps', 'rogues', 'vagabonds' and 'travellers'. Much of this legislation was designed to discourage their aimless way of life and to prevent them from becoming a burden on the community.

Those who fell into extreme poverty had to resort to the Poor Law Union, the chief state agency for the relief of the destitute. In practice this meant the local Board of Guardians, an elected body which levied an annual rate to alleviate the poverty of those it deemed worthy of assistance. For the entire Victorian period the support available to settled and vagrant poor was governed by the Poor Law Amendment Act of 1834, under which even the vagrant had settlement rights – the entitlement to support from the parish in which he was normally resident – provided he remained within the boundary of the Union to which his parish belonged. A regulation of 1837 further required Unions in England and Wales to provide food and shelter for the itinerant destitute – in addition to the settled – in return for paupers performing work. Able-bodied Scots had no right to relief of any kind.

Soon accommodation for vagrants became a standard part of every workhouse in England and Wales. Casuals, as the itinerant poor who presented themselves at the workhouse were known, first had to find one of the Union's relieving officers and seek admission. In the early years casuals were usually housed in infectious wards, separate from the main body of the workhouse: not only were vagrants known for carrying contagious diseases – notably measles – but they generally undermined the good order of the workhouse and were best kept away from other paupers. Eventually most workhouses developed purpose-built facilities to house them. Brick floors, iron 'guardroom' beds and the absence of heating gave the tramp ward a harsh institutional oppressiveness. They were also known as 'vagrant wards', 'casual wards' and 'the spike'.

As there were limited beds available, it was common for vagrants to start queuing outside the workhouse from late afternoon. The wards opened at about 5 or 6pm and vagrants were searched for money, tobacco and alcohol. Anyone with money was forced to pay; consequently they invariably hid their valuables outside before being searched, and retrieved them on release. The vagrants then stripped and bathed and were given a nightshirt and a blanket, while their clothes were 'stoved' or fumigated. Their supper consisted of 8oz of bread and a pint of gruel, known as 'skilly'. Sometimes it was a lump of cheese, a hunk of bread and gruel with only water to drink.

It was common for the police to ferry vagrants to the workhouse – which often turned them away. One of the young vagrant criminals Mayhew interviewed in 1850 maintained that it was pointless for the likes of him to apply to the parish as it invariably rejected the young and fit. A report by the Colchester Union explained one reason for turning vagrants away: to admit them often meant that 'every article in the room swarmed with vermin … The most horrible and loathsome diseases pervade most of them and it is by such persons that fevers and cutaneous [skin] disorders are communicated to the regular inmates.'

However, from 1837 unions were legally obliged to take vagrants – though this did not always happen. In order to qualify for a breakfast an allocated quota of work had to be completed. Often this involved stone breaking but many workhouses enforced different tasks. Salford workhouses, for instance, had a corn-grinding mill, operated by handles in the cells. After breakfast their fumigated clothes were returned and they were turned out for work. The old and infirm were excused labour and the unwell saw the workhouse medical officer, who might admit them to the infirmary. The fit were retained to work for no longer than four hours after breakfast. Those who arrived on Saturday were detained until Monday. There was no work on Sundays but the inmates were locked in their sleeping quarters all day where they talked, brooded and picked vermin from their clothes and bodies.

George Orwell recounted his experiences of a Sunday 'lock-in' during the 1930s. 'We leaned against the wall and the tramps began to talk about the spikes they had been in recently. It appeared from what they said that all spikes are different, each with their own peculiar merits and demerits, and it is important to know those when you are on the road.' There is no reason to believe that his experience was any different from that of tramps half a century earlier.

Workhouses took other measures to discourage the moocher. From 1871 those who appeared regularly – twice within a month – were liable not only to be detained but also required to perform tasks similar to those imposed on a criminal serving a prison sentence. This certainly deterred the moocher, as the number of people presenting themselves at casual wards fell to half the pre-1870 figure.

The Casual Poor Act of 1882 increased the workhouse powers of detention: first-time applicants could now be detained until the morning of the second day after arrival, while habituals might be held until the fourth day after arrival. For the purposes of the Act all London casual wards were deemed one unit: in other words, anyone presenting himself at two different workhouses in London within a single month could be detained at the second for three days and compelled to perform penal labour.

As with most aspects of the workhouse, there are conflicting accounts of the nature of inmates. One tramp, reflecting at the end of the nineteenth century on his experience of casual wards over many years, concluded that, while many inmates were 'moochers' – ne'er-do-wells – there were also some genuinely seeking work. A few years later, Patrick Macgill and his fellow tramping navvies – Moleskin Joe, Carroty Dan, Clancy of the Cross and Dermod Flynn – avoided the spikes, and indeed all private lodging houses and instead stuck to the 'models', which seems to support the view of a Poor Law official in a northern union who claimed that only about three per cent of causal ward inmates were genuinely seeking work, while the rest were hardened and incorrigible vagrants.

The standard of accommodation, spartan and functional as it was, was better than that offered by the average common lodging house. Tramp wards were certainly superior in cleanliness. Speaking of Flower and Dean Street, near where the Ripper murders occurred, J.E. Ritchie believed that 'in prisons and workhouses the inmates are much better lodged'. Yet few of those with personal experience of both agreed with this verdict. It's easy to see why the workhouse held no attractions for those able to afford the few coppers needed for a lodging house.

The rigorous discipline and enforced working regime of the workhouse was anathema to the habitual moocher. The abstemious life of the tramp ward, with its absence of women, drink and tobacco, was to the liking of few inmates. Besides, those the tramp major believed to have 'the Scratch' – scabies – were subjected to a 'brimstone bath' which involved the entire body being enclosed in a box, with a hole for the head, in which a quantity of brimstone was then burnt.

James Greenwood, having sampled the workhouse, later visited the lodging houses of Golden Lane, in the City, reputedly 'the very ugliest neighbourhood in all England' in 1874. He remarked that the people he encountered there were of the same class as those in the casual ward, though the atmosphere was totally different. He concluded that one of the greatest attractions of the lodging house was that there a man might go to bed as dirty as he likes – and there were few who did not take full advantage of this happy situation.

The same year Greenwood visited the 'hot water houses' of Little Cheapside, Cowheel Alley, Reform Place and Hot Water Place, where there were no beds but for a penny customers could lie on the floor with about twenty other beggars and cadgers. The people there expressed contempt for those who availed themselves of parish charity, dismissing them as 'idle loafers'. Even among the dregs of society there are gradations of ignominy as important to them as the distinctions between a baronet and a duke are to the aristocracy.

Another explanation for this aversion is suggested by Mayhew. After speaking to hundreds of vagrants, he was convinced that above all else they valued warmth and were prepared to sacrifice everything else for it. 'Otherwise,' he says, 'to sleep, or even sit in, some of the apartments of these establishments [common lodging houses] would be intolerable.' Besides, the enforced work task deterred the vagrant. Andrew Doyle's study of the casual wards in the West Midlands and Welsh Borders led him to conclude that three-quarters of the occupants were 'thieves of every sort, deserters from the army, bad characters of every sort … runaway apprentices and idle vagabonds of every kind', united only in their determination never to work. This fits in with a great deal of anecdotal evidence from those who spent time in lodging houses, where criminals and beggars were unanimous in their contempt for those foolish enough to work, dismissing them, regardless of age, as 'young mugs'.

Despite this strong aversion, there was no sharp division between many of those who used the lodging houses and the patrons of the tramp wards. Many itinerants used both. In London in the 1890s there was a shifting population of what Charles Booth called 'poor derelicts of humanity' who ebbed from common lodging houses to night shelters and flowed to tramp wards with the regularity of the turning tide. The numbers in lodging houses increased sharply during the winter of 1888 to 1889 as the number of organisations offering indiscriminate charity increased, thus attracting vagrants to the city, many of whom spent their days making the rounds of one charity after another, eating their fill and then returning to the lodging house where they sold their excess food and clothing or exchanged it for drink.

This was not confined to London or the big cities and towns. In Chester for instance, and other places where outdoor relief was easily had, many vagrants used it to pay for their lodgings. In St Thomas', Oxford, many of those who usually found shelter in the workhouse such as unmarried mothers, lone children, the disabled and those of advanced old age, were long-term residents of lodging houses and there is ample evidence that it was fairly common for such people and those supported by private charities to find a place in a lodging house.

Yet working people were also sometimes forced to use the casual wards. Seasonal farm workers, including fruit pickers, used those on their route to where they worked and while there lived in sheds and other forms of improvised shelter. The Kent and Sussex wards catered for many Londoners who were down for the hop-picking at the end of the summer. The seasonal migration of harvesters, many of them Irish, was a well-established part of the ebb and flow of population long before Victoria came to the throne. The Irish crossed over in the late summer, travelled to their place of work and returned home before the winter.

Of all those in search of temporary accommodation, none was the subject of more curiosity or attracted as much public discussion as the navvy. He attained mythical status during the nineteenth century as the vast engineering projects on which he worked eventually criss-crossed Britain with a network of roads, canals and railway lines and transformed the country. Many historians believe these structures are a greater achievement than the Pyramids or the Great Wall of China.

One of the things that made the nineteenth century navvy so conspicuous was his clothes, which were as distinctive as a judge's wig or a policeman's helmet. He wore a big donkey jacket, with two wide outside pockets and inside a large poacher's pocket. Moleskin or heavy corduroy trousers, a double-canvas shirt, a velvet or corduroy waistcoat, a billycock hat, a wide, big-buckled belt, to support his back when lifting, and a large scarf of coloured cotton, tied with a special 'pincher's knot', made up the rest of his attire. Just as the student of the 1960s hoping for a summer job on a building site betrayed his inexperience by wearing trainers, so the nineteenth-century navvy signalled his experience by wearing the correct uniform.

The first navvies were the men who built the 'inland navigation system', the canal system, between 1745 and 1830. People called them 'navigators' – later shortened to 'navvies' – a term that remained in popular and official use for two centuries. Later it came to describe any labourer who worked on large-scale civil engineering projects.

Initially, a significant number of these men were migrant agricultural labourers from the poorer parts of Ireland, often subsistence farmers from the north-west, west and south-west of Ireland. It was customary for people from these areas to travel to England to work on the harvest. Later, in the mid-nineteenth century, many Irishmen fled their famine-stricken land and came to England in search of work. When George Stephenson, John Rennie, James Brindley and other pioneering engineers recruited labour for their roads and canals, Irishmen signed up.

But the majority of navvies were not Irish. Many came from Britain's dispossessed rural population, driven out by enclosure and advances in agricultural practices which left no role for marginal farmers dependent on common land to eke out an existence. Others were labourers living in the areas adjacent to each civil engineering project. Some were the ancestors of the 15,000 travellers who live in Britain today. Nor were they all mobile: the majority of those who worked on the major engineering projects remained in the area when the project was completed.

But others – many of them young and unattached – moved on to the next job. They mastered the 'graft', a drain-digging spade which became the symbol of their trade, and formed part of an itinerant workforce to be found wherever major construction was going on.

As the century progressed navvies became a recognised and distinct section of the working population, set apart by the special nature of their work. They were rightly proud of their expertise. A good navvy could shift twenty tonnes of earth a day. Navvies new to the job could not keep up with the experienced workers and they frequently managed only a half-day's work. It took a year to gain the strength, stamina and experience required to perform feats of endurance which struck many contemporaries as super-human. Nor was the British navvy's reputation for prodigious labour confined to these shores. Many went on to work in Europe, where they frequently earned twice the pay of others because they were deemed twice as productive. Many travelled to America where they worked on canals and most famously the railways.

But their reputation had a less positive aspect. They were renowned for fighting, hard living and hard drinking. 'Respectable' Victorians viewed them as outside civilised society and feared for both their moral welfare and the bad example they set. Their fears were fuelled by incidents such as that in 1846, when the huts of Irish workers near Penrith were attacked and troops had to be called out after a riot ensued. The Navvy Mission Society was perhaps the greatest of the organisations tasked with their spiritual welfare.

Yet the navvies' were transforming the country. The 3,400 miles of canal built in Britain during the eighteenth and nineteenth centuries are a phenomenal achievement. Building a canal is more than just digging a big ditch. It involves quarrying, brick-making, joinery and iron working; laying rails and pipes; and building locks, bridges, gates, arches and tunnels. Navvies not only excavated the channel, moving millions of tons of soil with picks, shovels and wheelbarrows. They also lined the bottom and sides with impermeable clay, working it into position with the soles of their boots. This 'heeling-in' or 'puddling' process was used for 200 years. As recently as 1964 the Chew Valley Reservoir in the south-west of England was lined by the same method used on the Newry Canal in 1742.

In return for this the navvy commanded high wages. In 1845 he earned 3s 9d (19p) a day – twice the wage of a farm labourer. To maintain this income he had to be mobile and follow the work. During the years of the great railway boom of the mid-nineteenth century, professional navvies were the norm. In some areas local labourers supplemented their numbers, but on the major developments in urban areas or in remote, thinly populated regions, the seasoned navvy was the bedrock on which the railways were built. At one stage during the nineteenth century, one in every hundred workers was a navvy. During the height of railway construction in the mid-nineteenth century, more than 250,000 navvies were employed throughout Britain.

Moving from place to place to work on the large number of public works undertaken in Victorian Britain, many navvies found accommodation in lodging houses in nearby towns and villages. But they were often unwelcome guests as their reputation for dishonesty, drinking, womanising and riotous behaviour usually preceded them. Besides, there was never sufficient accommodation for the great armies of navvies on major schemes, and the result was that many slept in the open or in squalid shanties. Employers refused to incur the cost of decent accommodation and consequently many of these navvy settlements were struck by cholera, dysentery or typhus. The inevitable public outcry resulted in a gradual improvement and by the end of the nineteenth century contractors were obliged to provide their workers with adequate accommodation.

This, however, did nothing to reduce the dangers inherent in their work. Though deaths and serious injuries were commonplace, as late as the 1840s there was no compensation scheme and railway engineers like Brunel resisted all efforts to improve the safety of working conditions. It was only with the Woodhead Tunnel scandal that changes were made. The death rate among the navvies who built the tunnel, between 1839 and 1852, was higher than that of the soldiers who fought at the Battle of Waterloo. A parliamentary inquiry ensued and after many years its recommendations for improved safety procedures began to filter through to working practices.

The constant danger under which the navvy worked added to his aura and spread with the roads, canals and railways. They were the elite of the labouring class, the renowned 'long-distance men', who lived for the moment, taking risks and spending their wages riotously. Free of domestic ties, they lived rough and didn't care what people thought of them. Yet they were good-hearted, generous and loyal to their own and despite middle class fears, local newspaper in areas that had experience of them were often complimentary. Journalists had nothing but praise for the men building the Manchester Ship Canal between 1887 and 1894, commending them for their generosity and gentlemanly demeanour.

Building the famous canal was so dangerous and the company surgeon, Robert Jones, became so adept at making artificial limbs for disabled navvies that he is acknowledged as the father of orthopaedic surgery. In total, 2,000 men were disabled and 1,100 lost their lives constructing the waterway that made Manchester a great inland port.

The Ship Canal is only the most famous of the great public utilities which the navvies made their speciality. Between 1845 and 1853 alone they built seven major reservoirs in the Edinburgh area. The navvies working on the Manchester to Liverpool Railway received no pay when sick or injured. Instead their employer issued them with meal tokens, which they could exchange for bread and soup.

Travelling the length and breadth of the country in search of work, they built up a support network, usually based on public houses. Many of these hostelries, like the Mason's Arms and the Bricklayer's Arms, still bear the mark of their origins and are one of the reasons why navvies became associated with pubs and drink. This is not to say that this reputation was entirely undeserved, as the evidence of newspaper reports and anecdotal reportage is overwhelming. Navvies often received their wages in public houses, where their desire to celebrate met a convenient and immediate outlet. Men who were well-paid after a week of hard physical labour often found in the public house the conviviality and leisure they craved. Far from home and family, opportunities for recreation and relaxation were limited and the pub was one of the few places where they were sure of a warm welcome.

Warmth of another kind was what drew many to the lodging house.

Dot Dancing: The Kitchen Fire

Navvy or beggar, it made no difference: everyone who crossed the threshold of a lodging house expected a blazing fire to greet them. What happened when lodgers gathered around it was often not to the liking of commentators. Mary Higgs, for instance, describes with barely suppressed revulsion, what she witnessed when she entered a women's lodging house in the early years of the twentieth century. Clustered round the fire were 'a group of girls far gone in dissipation … shamelessly smoking cigarettes, boasting of drink and drinkers, using foul language, singing music hall songs and talking vileness. A girl called Dot danced the "cake-walk" in the middle of the kitchen.'

Despite the reservations of Mary Higgs, there were few who could resist Dot's dancing or the other pleasures that unfolded in front of the fire. No matter how squalid, impoverished and unwelcoming a lodging house, every keeper, even of those patronised exclusively by beggars, knew that a welcoming fire was an absolute necessity if he hoped to stay in business. Visiting a lodging house situated 'in a court within a court' near Drury Lane in 1844, John Fisher Murray wrote that despite all its deficiencies the house had 'a capital fire' and that 'the fire in these hotels is three parts of the accommodation'. When, as in this case, the house also provided a common saucepan, a gridiron and a frying pan, its clients were prepared to overlook virtually all other shortcomings. There, as in most such places, they were happy to sup their tea from a jam jar.

The fire was in every sense the centre of the lodging house. It was where the lodgers cooked, ate and congregated to gossip or exchange information. It was the centre of communal life, the place where people gathered to escape the cold and rain, to smoke and while away the hours, to wash, dry and mend their clothes. It was also an independent source of income for the keeper as those who were not lodgers were able, for a small fee, to utilise the kitchen all day, cook and make use of the boiling water always available for making tea and coffee. They stayed there out of the rain and cold. For a penny they also had use of the frying pan.

As late as the 1880s, writing of a lodging house in the Covent Garden area, James Greenwood, like many commentators before and after him, remarked that 'the most conspicuous feature of the house was the fire that blazed in a grate capacious enough to roast a whole sheep. It is easy to understand that it is regarded as no inconsiderable part of their money's worth by the poor, shivering wretches who of nights pay the fourpenny entrance fee.'

Describing the kitchens of the lodging houses in Saffron Hill in the mid-nineteenth century, Beams likens them to the tap room of a low public house, where the most disgusting conversation took place. Not all, however, took part in these discussions. Many were busy cooking, others were reading and drowsing, while more sat around smoking. In such places people smoked even in the sleeping areas, despite which there were surprisingly few fires, probably because there were so many lodgers awake and moving about at all times of the day and night. Though Victorian men did not smoke in the presence of respectable women – let alone curse – the air in the lodging house was thick with both obscenities and tobacco smoke for, whatever their station in life or their expectations, lodgers were united in their love of tobacco. Smoking was for many itinerants their greatest luxury and the height of self-indulgence. As Mayhew put it, in such places 'anyone who was not hardened to tobacco smoke was half-killed with coughing.'

Conversation was liveliest in houses frequented by thieves and prostitutes. These are the places Mayhew refers to when he speaks of 'the habitual violation of all injunctions of law, of all obligations of morality and of all restraints of decency'. Surprisingly, he was convinced that such places were more often run by women than men.

However, the hearth also had a severely practical function. As Mayhew put it, 'In lodging houses every sojourner is his own cook', and the commonest meal was tea with a piece of bacon or the ubiquitous herring, a staple of the urban poor, or haddock, bloaters and sausage. The better kitchens provided most things required to cook and eat a meal with the exception of cutlery, which was easily stolen and too dangerous to make available to lodgers. Each lodger had to have his own crockery or utensils or else hire them and those who could not afford such luxuries ate with their hands from newspaper. The kitchen also served as a laundry and drying room, a workshop where clothes and boots were repaired and a barber's.

Though to the casual observer lodgers were indistinguishable, closer scrutiny and first-hand experience revealed that this was far from the case. Though the occupants of lodging houses could not avoid close physical proximity with fellow lodgers, they usually socialised with their own type. Beggars seldom mixed with burglars: a social divide as wide as that between a duchess and a dustman separated them in the hierarchy of the lodging house. Yet both looked down on those who worked for a living.

There was also a tacit understanding that lodgers valued their anonymity. They were not required to provide a name and even long-term residents often preferred it that way. Many used pseudonyms. Among the West Midlands patrons of lodging houses in 1866 nicknames included: Saucy Harry and his moll, Bristol Jack and Burslem, Harry the Mark from Carmarthen, Spanish Jim, Hungerford Tom and Stockport Ginger, the Governor of Chester Castle, Belfast Jack, Wakefield Charley and Lancashire Crab. Other lodgers of the same period travelled under the names of William Outlaw, Huzza King, William Shakespeare, Abraham Lincoln, Patrick Skibbereen and William Gladstone. A bricklayer and a carpet weaver, who were travelling companions, gave their names at their Hereford lodging house in 1861 as Necodemous Salt and Michael Pepper.

In the lowest lodging houses around London docks which Mayhew visited in 1849 the kitchens generally opened at 5am and closed at 11pm, at which time a fresh batch of lodgers was taken in and those who had slept there the previous night turned out. This was often a cause of trouble and frequently violence. Attempts by those without the means to stay to gatecrash or 'bilk' a spot near the fire were a recurring problem. To prevent this from happening many keepers locked the doors to the sleeping area and the outside doors of the house, despite the dangers of fire. Dealing with objectionable lodgers could involve the use of force and, as no lodging house welcomed the involvement of the police, owners often employed ex-boxers to deal with disagreeable customers.

Though keepers and lodgers did not always agree, the latter were occasionally capable of collective acts of generosity which encapsulate all that was best and most attractive about the lodging house. James Greenwood witnessed what was known among those who lived in lodging houses in the 1880s as 'a bunker'. It was really a banquet benefit, a meal organised by the lodgers for the purpose of raising money for one of their number who was in urgent need of cash.

The food was provided by beggars, who went from house to house asking for something to eat. Even the most hard-hearted householders – or more often their servants – who refused to give beggars money could often be wheedled into giving them food. The beggars then collected what they had begged and divided it up into parcels which they sold, usually to other lodgers. The rest was made up into a hotchpotch stew. The lodgers then bought – for 6*d* – the right to eat as much as they could consume and the proceeds went to the person in need.

When the feast Greenwood describes was about to commence it became clear that some lodgers, lacking the necessary 6*d*, were to be excluded. One of these, whose eyes looked ravenously on the food, was a street musician whose entire wardrobe consisted of a tattered coat too small for him, fastened at the throat with a piece of twine, a pair of trousers and broken down mismatched shoes, through the front of one of which his naked toes were visible. This man had to make do with the penny parcel of begged food, which he ate out of his cap. 'His cheeks were sunk so close together it seemed a marvel how he could shut his mouth without biting them.' The beneficiary received 15*s* and 6*d*.

As the lodging house was capable of fostering such camaraderie and producing a mutual support system which encouraged ingenuity and self-help, why was it so universally feared and denounced by commentators? Why was it talked of in the same breath as psychotic depravity and brutal murder?

Chapter Three

'Stains on the Walls and Floorboards': The Location of Lodging Houses

Some crimes are so vile that time fails to diminish their capacity to appal. Others retain a grim fascination because they encapsulate a particular place at a specific time and are redolent of a world that has passed away. A few continue to enthral because they provide a tantalising glimpse into the disordered mind of the homicidal psychopath, yet remain an insoluble puzzle. A small number combine all these elements; these become the focus of intense and enduring fascination: details are sifted and dissected, held up to the light and examined from every possible angle. Such are the Ripper murders which took place in Whitechapel in 1888, the year in which snow fell on London in July.

Of all the countless details of the Ripper murders brought to light by those who have examined the case, one in particular provides an insight into the world of the East End where the crimes were committed. In fact, this detail does not relate to the actual murders but to the situation years after the Ripper had disembowelled Mary Kelly, his final victim.

Four years after that night of 9 November, on which the Ripper butchered his fifth victim, a reporter went to the house in Miller's Court where the murder took place. He found the house and the rented room where Mary Kelly suffered such an excruciating death. Lottie Owens, the new tenant, let him in.

As soon as he entered the room he saw them: enormous liver-coloured stains across the walls and the bare floorboards. There was no doubt about it: this was Mary's congealed blood. The landlord had not thought it necessary to redecorate the room.

The area in which Jack the Ripper found his victims was quintessential lodging house land. On the nights they were murdered, two of his victims – Mary Nichols and Annie Chapman – were evicted from their lodging houses for want of a few coppers to pay for a bed. Three of the Ripper's victims had at one time lived in the same lodging house. We know a lot about this area and not simply because of the murders: the neighbourhood to the east and west of Commercial Road, Whitechapel, where all the victims lived, had for many years been the subject of intense interest to social reformers. In particular, the common lodging house and its denizens were of endless fascination to both the serious investigator and those in search of grim stories with which to titillate the readers of broadsheets and the yellow press.

Long before 1888, the year of the Ripper, this area was infamous for crime and in particular violent crime, to such an extent that only criminals dared venture there even during the day. No policeman dared enter alone. In a small area bounded by Baker's Row, Middlesex Street and Whitechapel Road virtually every house was a lodging house, 146 in total, with over 6,000 beds. Over 1,500 of these were in Flower and Dean Street alone, with nearly 700 in Dorset Street. Flower and Dean Street was described by one social commentator as 'perhaps the foulest and most dangerous street in the whole metropolis'. The average tenant in a Dorset Street lodging house was a man between the ages of 20 and 40, working in the docks, the nearby Covent Garden Market or on a building site – all of which offered opportunities for pilfering, with the result that the area was awash with stolen goods.

The houses ranged from private homes that took in a few lodgers to enormous buildings which accommodated as many as 350 people. Some of these were single sex but the majority were known as 'double-class beds' and were the haunts of prostitutes. Of Dorset Street's 1,078 inhabitants in 1871, 902 lived in 31 lodging houses.

Hugh Edward Hoare, director of Hoares' Brewery, who represented West Cambridge as MP from 1892 to 1895 and took over the running of a lodging house in this area, was a perceptive observer who expressed succinctly what many others hinted at in the *Cambridge Independent Press* beginning on 14 September 1888. What struck him most forcefully was not the physical squalor but the ethos these streets exuded: 'I was perfectly conscious of a different moral atmosphere.' When he first turned into the street, he both saw and felt this difference. 'A feeling comes over you that you can do as you like, you become aware of a disposition to throw open your coat, to pull out your pipe and put your hands in your pockets and the hat on the back of your head.'

In 1888, a rented room at 26 Dorset Street cost 4*s* 6*d* a week. Furnishings inside the 10ft square room consisted of a bed, two small tables, a clothes horse and a storage cupboard. Heat and cooking facilities were provided by an open fire. The floor was of bare boards and, as there were neither blinds nor curtains, the window was obscured by clothing hanging from the curtain rail. This room was home to Joe Barnett and his paramour, Mary Kelly. Joe lost his job and could no longer afford to pay the rent, forcing Mary into prostitution. She became the Ripper's fifth and final victim.

Mary Anne Nicholls, known as Polly, could not afford such a room. As a broken down, alcoholic prostitute, even the few coppers required for a bed in the lodging house near the junction of Thrall Street and Flower and Dean Street were beyond her means on the night she was murdered. Turned out onto the street, she went in search of someone prepared to pay sixpence for her body.

Annie Chapman's situation was identical to Polly's. Her husband had turned her out because of her drinking and she fell into prostitution, spending the money she did not drink on a bed in McCarthy's lodging house at 30 Dorset Street. She had recently left there and moved the short distance to Crossingham's lodging house at 35 Dorset Street. On the night she was murdered she was thrown out as she had no money.

Three doors along from Crossingham's was another lodging house, number 38, owned by Jack McCarthy. The reputation of the houses in this street was abominable. Such was the hostility to them that at the height of the Ripper terror, in October 1888, the wife of a local clergyman presented a petition to Queen Victoria signed by 4,000 'Women of Whitechapel' beseeching her to close them all. The houses remained open, but the Home Office asked the local police to provide information on prostitution in the area and in particular the extent to which lodging houses were involved. The police return showed that in the area to the east and west of Commercial Road there were 233 lodging houses, with accommodation for 8,530, and 62 brothels. They estimated that there were 1,200 prostitutes in the locality, most of whom were of 'the lowest condition'.

The Rookeries – 'The Night Time Haven of the Wandering Tribes'

This entire area of the East End was what one contemporary described as 'the night time haven of the wandering tribes'. Lodgers made up the bulk of the wandering tribes and were of two types: the transient and the 'regulars'. The same mixture seems to have been found in lodging houses everywhere and just as those in Whitechapel were in the worst houses in the worst areas of the city so were those to be found in cities and towns elsewhere. In Leicester at this time, for instance, many of the town's most dilapidated old timber buildings were lodging houses.

Similarly, one of the most infamous clusters of Manchester lodging houses was centered on Charter Street, in Angel Meadow, which was within a short distance of the sprawling Manchester cotton mills. Over half this area's residents in 1851 lived in lodging houses and were professional or occasional criminals, 'well-known to the police throughout the kingdom', according to Angus Bethune Reach. The worst streets were Charter Street, the main thoroughfare, Blakeley (Bleakley) Street and Dantzig Street. In 1865 the police found the area swarming with crowds of known thieves, sometimes up to a hundred strong, who gathered during the middle of the day.

A number of feared criminals dominated the area. One such was Joe Hyde, who ran the London Tavern, a meeting place for criminals from all over the country. Nearby, Teddy Bob Butterworth provided accommodation in his lodging houses for professional rogues of every description. The area was also home to three of Manchester's most prominent fences – Bob Macfarlane, One-armed Kitty and Cabbage Ann – who constituted the means by which thieves disposed of much of the swag that sloshed around the area.

What all these places had in common was that they were the oldest parts of the city, with the worst housing and near sources of unskilled, casual employment. Pubs, beerhouses and lodging houses shouldered each other in this tangle of streets and courtyards. These were archetypal rookeries.

The term 'rookery' was widely used in the eighteenth and nineteenth centuries to refer to a part of the city that was not just run down and squalid but also the haunt of criminals and prostitutes. These were honeycombed with small alleys and narrow streets, the complexity of which could be used by miscreants to evade arrest. Rookeries were places into which criminals could escape and often the hole in which they took refuge was a lodging house.

The term 'slum' which, courtesy of the town planners and the politically correct, now sounds both archaic and objectionable, is of 1820s vintage. One part of mid-nineteenth century Leeds provides another good example of a slum. Packed into an area 400m from the parish church, there were 222 lodging houses, home to 2,500 people, with an average of 2.5 people per bed and 4.5 to a room. When cholera struck the city in 1851 public health officials traced its origins to this area. Joseph Dare found that in Leicester at the same time the majority of the city's lodging houses were concentrated in the oldest and most dilapidated areas, particularly St Margaret's. Studies of lodging houses in Cardiff, Wolverhampton and Huddersfield all show that they were concentrated in central districts, where there was an abundance of suitably large and cheap buildings.

In 1899 Charles Booth identified the other rookeries of London. He cited St Giles, Jacob's Island and Old Nichol Street, all three of which were demolished at the end of the nineteenth century as part of the slum clearance scheme. The Devil's Acre, a notorious area near Westminster

Abbey, was one of the first places to which the term 'slum' was applied. Clustered around Old Pye Street, which was lined with lodging houses, it became known as the 'Irish Rookery'. The 1851 census records that in one of these houses, fifteen of the twenty occupants were Irish; five described themselves as beggars, two as beggar bricklayers, one a labourer beggar, one a needlewoman beggar, one a hawker, one a labourer bricklayer and one an errand boy.

The potteries and piggeries of Notting Hill made no pretence to respectability and gloried in the epithet 'Cutthroat Lane'. In 1850 Dickens described it as 'a plague pot scarcely equalled for its insalubrity by any other in London'. Saffron Hill in Camden was in 1850 a squalid neighbourhood, home to paupers and thieves. Dickens located Fagin's den in Field Lane, a southern extension of Saffron Hill.

With so many areas vying for notoriety there developed a competition between commentators, each claiming to have uncovered the worst rookery in the city or in the entire country. While there were plenty of obvious candidates, there were also unexpected contenders, their claims advanced by experienced observers. One such, proffered by Mr Walker, a City Missionary of vast experience, was the Berwick Street district of St James's in the mid-nineteenth century. This area he said was 'one of the most vicious districts which blot the map of the metropolis – a busy nursery of vice and crime, and the very focus of the kingdom's worst criminality. Wretchedness and ruin appear on every side. Neither Whitechapel nor St Giles's could vie with it in the scenes of depravity it could exhibit.' This area is worth describing in some detail as, even allowing for Walker's gift for hyperbole, its features are typical of virtually all the rookeries in every British city of the time.

The district contained 190 houses:

which appear encrusted with the filth and smoke of generations, twenty-four lodging-houses and seven pubs. The population is around 3,000, most of whom seemed to be on the streets most of the time, hanging about in groups, half-dressed, unwashed, loitering in doorways, leaning out of derelict windows or at the end of narrow courts, smoking, swearing and occasionally fighting, their children filthy and swarming about their feet naked and neglected.

Burglars, pickpockets, coiners, passers of counterfeit money and every type of criminal seemed to have their headquarters in the district and the remainder of the population were beggars and hucksters.

Every house appeared to be packed to capacity with reprobates of all hues. New Court, for instance, contained twelve houses, each made up of six rooms, and in one house alone seventy-two people were living. From this same house, over a period of three months, sixty-nine young people were transported (to an Australian penal colony) and one inhabitant was executed at Newgate. Walker also reported that he had 'seen upward of forty policemen beaten out of this street by the inhabitants while attempting to take a thief'.

The King Street rookery in Southampton and the London Road area of Manchester enjoyed a similar reputation. A police survey of the latter at the end of the nineteenth century provides a vivid picture of life in the area. Shepley Street, just off London Road, was typical. Numbers 8 and 10 were brothels. Numbers 22 and 26 were common lodging houses, separated by the Rose and Crown, the haunt of prostitutes. However, the police report reveals something that none of the commentators mention or even hint at: on these same streets lived many respectable labourers, skilled craftsmen and shopkeepers. Invariably these people were struggling to live honest and useful lives, seeking to distance themselves from known criminals.

It is noteworthy that even in areas such as this, the population was never clearly divisible into the respectable and the criminal. Mixed up with the honest workers, professional criminals and the recent immigrants trying to scrape a living in an alien environment, were large numbers of people who lived in a twilight zone between legitimate society and the underworld. They drifted between these two worlds, never entirely sure where one ended and the other began. Most of this amorphous group consisted of those who never enjoyed the benefits of regular employment but survived only because they were able to pick up occasional jobs. Many sometimes worked as hawkers, knife-grinders, ballad singers and sellers of broadsheets.

In county towns lodging houses were concentrated in areas close to sources of employment for lodgers. In Daventry, Northamptonshire, for instance, lodging houses were clustered around Brook Street, where local businesses included a bone collector, a dealer in old iron and an umbrella-maker – all occupations commonly found among lodgers. In the vicinity of Baker Street, the focus of Shrewsbury's lodging houses, were a sugar boiler, marine-store dealers and second-hand clothes dealers. Adjacent to Banbury's largest lodging house was a one-legged old soldier who manufactured matches – which many of the lodgers subsequently hawked. This pattern was replicated throughout the country.

From the 1850s onwards, the economic situation of those in irregular employment, never better than precarious, was also declining relative to their neighbours in permanent employment. Factory workers' incomes were generally improving, however. Whole leisure and consumer industries – notably the pub and the music hall – grew up to meet the needs of working men with money. It was this coming together of criminals, wanderers, the honest poor, those whose economic position was improving and large numbers of immigrants which gave the slums their multi-faceted character.

Unlike today, when a great deal of official language seems designed to conceal reality and to promote 'non-judgmental' attitudes, the Victorians tended to use terms which made their attitudes clear. Thus by the 1880s common lodging houses, home to about 50,000 Londoners who lived in these places more or less permanently, were often known as 'low lodging houses'. As Mayhew remarks, this term partly referred to the small charge paid by lodgers and partly to the character of their clients. He does, however, acknowledge that many lodging houses did not deserve this term in its opprobrious sense. He lists seventeen areas in the capital where these houses are to be found in great abundance and five areas were there are many of them – all within the poorest parts of the city and which yet contained many good lodging houses occupied chiefly by working people. Examples include those in Orchard Street, Westminster and the Mint.

Yet it is indisputable that conditions in the worst lodging houses were depressing. Many were tiny, distinguishable from private houses only by their dirtier exteriors and the fact that their windows often contained more paper than glass. Such signs were easily read by those seeking shelter who immediately realised that thieves and prostitutes were welcome. 'Some of them are of the worst class of low brothels,' Mayhew claimed, 'and some may even be described as brothels for children.' The better sort of street sellers and traders immediately knew to go elsewhere.

In such places in the 1850s bed generally consisted of a mattress of strong canvas stuffed with the worst cotton flocks, two sheets and a rug or leather sheet. It was known for the sheets to remain unchanged for three months. Changed frequently or not, they were all infested with vermin: Mayhew claims he 'never met an exception'. A pail in the middle of the room 'to which both sexes may resort' was the sole toilet facility available. One of Mayhew's informants told him, 'I myself have slept in the top room of a house not far from Drury Lane, and you could study the stars through the holes blown off the roof'. This, however, turned out to be an advantage for 'the room wasn't as foul as it might have been without them'. In other places he had 'scraped handfuls of bugs from bed clothes and crushed them under a candlestick many a time.' He often slept in a room that could barely hold twelve, with thirty others where the odour of their bodies rose 'in one foul, choking steam of stench'.

Overcrowding was often at its worst when local attractions drew great crowds of punters including those hoping to batten on unwary spectators. Everything from the Greenwich Fair to the Epsom Derby meant that the only available accommodation at local lodging houses involved sleeping with two or three strangers in a bed intended for one. On such occasions the space between beds would be filled with shake-downs or people sleeping on the floor. In the better houses these emergency beds were small palliasses or mattresses, whereas in the worst they were often no more than bundles of rags. In rural areas loose straw was commonly used.

When houses were packed to bursting, it was common for lodgers to sleep on the kitchen floor, which was often stone, without any bedding. This saved the lodger a penny. 'The Irish,' Mayhew remarked, 'at harvest time, often resort to this mode of passing the night.'

The cholera outbreak of 1854 had, Mayhew believed, one very beneficial effect: it frightened even vagrants into insisting that beds and bedding were improved. Yet standards remained low in many areas. Mayhew's informants in the 1850s assured him that the most unpleasant houses were to be found in London and the worst of these for both filth and the infamy of its lodgers were in the area around Drury Lane. The places they referred to were no more than gaunt barns, with punctured roofs, where lodgers were charged 3*d* a night.

The immorality that was common in these places was also frequently remarked on. Curiously in this context the Irish, who feature prominently in all accounts of lodging houses and who were blamed for so many ills, were held up as models of propriety: in Mayhew's words, 'Of all the people who resort to these places the Irish are far the best for chastity.'

Another of Mayhew's 1850 informants told him that 'fights and fierce fights are frequent in them and I have often been afraid murder would have been done'. Many other social investigators remarked on the prevalence of violence, which was as pervasive as the reek of the privies in most lodging houses. All lived in fear as irrational, drink-fuelled assaults were common. Peddlers were often robbed of their stock or takings and disagreements about food were frequent. This is one respect in which things had improved considerably by the advent of the twentieth century. Jack London's 1902 account *The People of the Abyss* testifies to this and he notes that the ever-present fear of violence was a thing of the past, as lodgers passed their time playing draughts and cards.

Where there was violence there was sure to be drink also. Drink was consumed in the majority of houses at all times of day and night, even when rules forbade it. This seems to have been the case even in model houses, as is recounted in Patrick Macgill's recollections of a tramping navvy.

Yet there is considerable evidence that those who still clung to respectability confined themselves to those houses which admitted only the sober and relatively clean. In some of these blacking brushes were supplied without charge and pen, paper and ink and soap were available, while for a small charge it was possible to hire a razor. Even among houses that catered especially for 'travellers' some were beyond reproach. Such was Farm House in the Mint, with 40 rooms, over 200 beds, 3 kitchens and a reading room, in which lodgers paid a penny to read the newspaper. Here, as in all well-ordered houses, it was common not to admit lodgers after midnight. One experienced lodger even told Mayhew of men there kneeling to say their prayers and enthused that 'it's wholesome and sweet enough there, and large separate beds'.

There is evidence that during the second half of the nineteenth century there was a steady improvement even in many seamen's lodging houses and in once infamous areas. Writing in 1881 Richard Rowe provides an account of the Highway in Ratcliff, an area known for its many seamen's lodging houses and which was once notorious but said to have improved in recent times. He visited a lodging house on the Whitechapel Road, near the docks, which was a converted sugar works with 300 beds. It was freshly limewashed and every lodger was required to wash before going to bed. The kitchen – in addition to the requisite blazing fire, kept going day and night – housed lockers for the lodgers' goods and had plenty of tables and forms. It was well ventilated and the bedding was sufficient. This was only one of the respectable houses in the Flower and Dean Street area.

Some of the inmates of these better houses lived there for years, paying on a weekly or half-weekly basis, whereas the chance caller was required to pay nightly. The former paid 2s a week and the latter 4d a night. All these registered houses posted details of the number of beds allowed in each room.

Yet, despite overwhelming evidence that the quality of lodging houses was not uniformly deplorable and that even in the worst areas they improved as the century wore on, the attitude of the political elite remained as intemperate as the lives of those who inhabited the worst houses. Those who did most to bring lodging houses to the notice of the public were invariably vehement in their condemnation of what they regarded as subversive institutions which served to undermine every conceivable facet of national well-being.

Mayhew, writing to the *Morning Chronicle* in 1850, set the tone for subsequent diatribes. He was convinced that 'vagrancy is largely due to and indeed chiefly maintained by low lodging houses'. But this was as nothing as compared to their major effects: 'Prisons, tread-mills, penal settlements, gallows – all are in vain – and ragged schools and city missions are of no avail as preventives of crime, so long as these wretched dens of infamy, brutality and vice continue their daily and nightly work of demoralisation.' In case anyone was still unclear about their impact, Mayhew added his view that 'at present they are not the preparatory schools but the finishing academies for every kind of profligacy and crime'.

Public fascination with the slums or rookeries and the lodging houses which seemed to epitomise many of their evils came to a head in the 1880s and culminated in the media frenzy surrounding the Jack the Ripper murders of 1888. Books and articles poured from the presses with lurid titles such as *How the Poor Live* and *Horrible London*. The *Pall Mall Gazette* regaled its readers with extracts from *The Bitter Cry of Outcast London*, Andrew Mearns' sensationalist account of East End life in which he informed readers that 'incest is common and no form of vice or sensuality causes surprise or attracts attention. The low parts of London are the sink into which the filth and abomination from all parts of the country seem to flow.'

Nor was it solely sensationalist journalists who expressed revulsion: serious social investigators and reformers abhorred lodging houses. Lord Ashley described them in 1848 as 'haunts of pollution', both physical and moral. A few years later in 1851, Mayhew called them 'wretched dens of infamy, brutality and vice'. In the opinion of Alsager Hay Hill they were 'seed beds of mendacity and vagabondage'. It is significant that in 1844 they became the first working class dwellings to be subjected to parliamentary controls.

As we saw earlier, it was as the seed-bed of infectious diseases that the slums became the object of middle class fears. But cholera was only one of the tramp-borne diseases that spread panic. Typhus, known as the 'Irish fever', was commonly associated with the Famine Irish, who, it was claimed, turned lodging houses into breeding grounds of disease. This is one of the reasons why casuals were separated from the workhouse regulars and also why they were not allowed to attend religious services in the workhouse.

From about 1850, when the fear of typhus was dissipating, the fear of smallpox carried by tramps took its place. 'For almost every town,' Chadwick said, 'the common lodging-houses are pointed out as the foci of contagious diseases throughout the district.' Scientific evidence suggests that mingling the clothes of inmates – as occurred when they were fumigated – and the sharing of bath water were likely to facilitate the spread of the disease. About half the outbreaks during the epidemic of 1893 originated with tramps.

This theme was echoed again and again into the twentieth century, as lodging houses – often bracketed with dog kennels and bone yards – were identified as a threat to public health and a source of smallpox. The consensus about the public health dangers was strongest when epidemics raged, particularly in 1848–9, 1866 and 1871–2. As early as 1848 the Leicester Domestic Mission became the first of numerous concerned groups to press for the closure of all lodging houses.

There were also frequent official reports linking tramps with syphilis, a disease most frequently fatal when neglected and allowed to reach its tertiary stage. The build-up of deposits of bone inside the sufferer's skull produces pressure on the brain, resulting in convulsions and paralysis. Occasionally the cartilage of the larynx falls in and the sufferer dies of asphyxiation.

Insanitary conditions were not only injurious to health: they undermined respectability, a key concept in the Victorian psyche, no less important to the poor than other classes. Working class women waged an unequal battle against dirt, striving to keep their children clean and maintain a home that was tidy and sanitary. Cleanliness was a key facet of the respectability for which working people strived and was deemed a reliable indicator of decency and moral propriety. There was a sense in which working people believed that cleanliness was literally next to godliness.

The lodging house made cleanliness almost impossible. A water butt often constituted the entirety of its washing facilities. With neither soap nor a towel, the lodger could do no more than give himself a swill in dirty water and then dry himself on his clothes. One informant in 1842 told the sanitary inspector, 'I have known the bedding to be left unchanged for three months … They are infested with vermin – I never met with an exception.' The inevitable result was that inadequate facilities and low standards 'led to lodgers losing all care about cleanliness'.

By the mid-nineteenth century it was a truism that the lodging houses were one of the pillars on which criminality rested. The Police Commissioner, Captain Hay, described them in his 1853 report as 'infamous brothels, harbours of criminals'. When, in 1862, the Manchester press again investigated the city's lodging houses they found that their moral character had not changed since Reach had ventured into Angel Meadow twenty years before. The same ragbag of fallen humanity lived there: prostitutes, their bullies, vagrants, cadgers, tramps, thieves and the low Irish huddled together in moral and physical squalor.

It was universally accepted too that children who lived in lodging houses were inevitably drawn into criminality and vice. Stories of the corruption wrought by the lodging house on the innocent country bumpkin, wide-eyed and bemused on her first encounter with the great metropolis, were legion. Such young women, it was generally believed, were inevitably sucked into prostitution if their first encounter with the city was the lodging house.

In their capacity to corrupt, even the better lodging houses were not beyond reproach. In his letters to the *Morning Chronicle* in 1850, Mayhew tells of a character he encountered in one of the most respectable lodging houses. His story was typical of a whole class of rogues who were not born into criminality but jumped into it because they wanted to 'see life'. He admitted that his family were good and kind, yet he ran away from home and joined a criminal gang, all of whom were transported to Australia. He became a pickpocket and then graduated to forging banknotes and later to using loaded dice to con people at race meetings. He committed highway robbery before his exploits as a forger resulted in a sentence of fourteen years' penal servitude. Yet, after seven he escaped and returned to England, where he lived in lodging houses which he described as the 'grand encouragement and concealment of crime'.

Their effect, according to Mary Higgs, was to 'exert suction for evil on the young girl and the young boy. They form plague spots.' The reason for this was quite simply because they 'concentrate those who prey on society.' As the nineteenth century drew to an end, the focus of social commentators was changing. Rather than deliberate on the physical conditions of the lodging houses, which were generally improving, it was the moral condition of the residents that attracted most attention.

Some writers also saw in the lodging house a threat to the established political order. Many observers remarked that its clients were invariably anti-establishment, vitriolic in their condemnation of the aristocracy and hostile to the monarchy. Howard Goldsmid saw in the unemployed, who in 1885 bemoaned their fate in lodging house kitchens up and down the land, the harbingers of revolution. In reality the political attitudes of the lodging house were cynical and disenchanted, tending towards the same disengagement from politics which is common among large sections of the British population today. Far from being convinced that they could replace the political system with a better one, they were defeatist and resigned in the extreme, too preoccupied with keeping body and soul together to concern themselves with wider issues.

Dick Turpin, Jack Sheppard and other legendary desperados were young criminals' heroes. They swapped tales of their legendary audacity around lodging house fires and in prison cells and sang about them in the pubs, beerhouses and penny gaffs they frequented. From the mid-century hawkers sold written accounts of their exploits. Yet there is no evidence that there was a camaraderie of the outcast or any sense of shared political interests. If any general social principle united lodgers it was an implicit belief in social Darwinism, the conviction that life consists of endless struggle and that only the ruthless survive.

Few nineteenth century commentators wrote of the depredations of the lodging house without mentioning the Irish and thereby appealing to the anti-Irish and particularly the anti-Catholic bigotry endemic to all sections of English society. From the early nineteenth century, and particularly during the great influx of Famine Irish after 1848, squalid accommodation was invariably associated with the Irish, whose lodging houses in the big cities were usually depicted as appalling. It is also true that many lodging houses were in the hands of Irish owners, perhaps as many as one in five, concentrated in areas with a larger Irish population. Their ownership tended to be greater in the west of the country, rather than the east, but the Irish-owner was to be found all over Britain, including rural areas where Irish agricultural labourers had worked in the years before the Famine.

Ramsey, a small Fenland market town with a population of only 2,461 in 1851, provides a good example. The largest lodging house in the area was owned by John Hall from County Longford, who accommodated thirty-seven lodgers, all but five of whom were Irish. The situation was similar in St Ives, Bourne, St Neot's, Gainsborough, Shrewsbury and throughout Shropshire. Newport, on the main route from Ireland to London and the Midlands, had eleven Irish lodging houses in 1851. In all instances Irish owners attracted their countrymen as lodgers. It was not without justification that the indigenous population regarded the Irish as extremely clannish.

A succinct summary of the range of woes associated with the common lodging house appears in the *Pictorial Handbook of London* in the mid-nineteenth century: 'The common lodging house is a disgrace to a Christian country, and a constant source of physical and moral evil. They are hotbeds of vice and crime, a disgrace to humanity.' Lodging houses were not merely seen as places where the degraded incorrigibles wallow in their depravity, but as traps waiting for those who are unfortunate enough to become entangled in their pernicious influence: 'it is to such sinks of iniquity and contamination that the newcomer takes abode on first arriving in [the city], or when quitting the parental roof, and there has every good principle undermined by evil associates until he becomes a pest to society.' Writing in 1909 Mary Higgs agreed, though there is no doubt that by then facilities had improved beyond all recognition. She maintained that 'conditions are allowed in common lodging houses that are a shame and a disgrace to civilization'.

This undiluted antipathy is partly due to the fact the common lodging house was something of great symbolic importance in Victorian society representing the antithesis of that revered institution, the family. Today we are constantly lectured that 'families come in all shapes and sizes', which in effect means that virtually any combination of individuals may designate itself a family. The Victorians believed otherwise. As the 1871 census stated, 'The natural family is founded by marriage, and consists, in its complete state, of husband, wife and children.' But the family was more than an objective norm: it was, as one historian put it, 'a state of mind' and an ideal to which all other arrangements were compared and invariably found wanting.

To Victorians it was self-evident that children who lacked parents were in peril – moral, financial and social. The family was the basis of a sound society, the means by which children were socialised and made useful citizens. The family was the ideal context within which women cherished their offspring, safe in the knowledge that their husband was there to provide economic security. Parental love, filial piety, self-sacrifice, religious faith, moral formation, loyalty and mutual support were all nurtured and encouraged within the family unit. Families were conducive to both the welfare of their members and society in general.

Given that no one seriously disputed this, why did so many Victorians of marriageable age live outside the warm embrace of the family?

Chapter Four

Fighting with a Dog:
Precarious Employment

In Graham Greene's novel *The Power and the Glory* the priest protagonist seeks shelter in an abandoned farm estate, absconded by its owners with only their dying dog left behind. Exhausted, starving and almost broken by the relentless pursuit of those sworn to murder him, he is desperate for something to eat. The dog has the only food available, scraps of meat on a bone, lying between its paws. Tormented by hunger, he forsakes all dignity and fights the dog for the meat.

There were many in Victorian Britain who knew how the priest felt. It was their daily lot. For most of the nineteenth century the average wage of an unskilled labourer was below subsistence level. Unlike current definitions of poverty, which classify those without a car or a personal computer as poor, these people did not earn enough to buy the food, clothes and shelter necessary to remain healthy. Many were dependent on lodging houses.

The problem for millions of Victorians was that they were locked into unequal competition with droves of others desperate for work. This was not only in a few areas of employment: all unskilled labourers were in this invidious position. Dockers were the most obvious example: there were at least thirty per cent more men trying to make a living on the docks than were employed at the peak of demand. In every port, from London to Glasgow and Liverpool to Hull, there were dock-side lodging houses whose residents depended on employment that was never better than precarious.

Dockers, however, were only one of the numerous groups condemned to a daily struggle to feed themselves. Large swathes of the working population found themselves in a similar situation: market workers, builders, barbers, chimney sweeps, scavengers, firewood choppers, hawkers and cabmen, sandwich men and envelope addressers. Below even these were people engaging in occupations of last resort, who existed in a permanent state of destitution, a meal away from starvation: the bone-grubbers, the rag-collectors, the crossing-sweepers and the messengers. Yet the dock worker was perhaps the most extreme example of employment that was insecure. They were taken on daily, if required, and invariably found that those competing with them for a day's work increased in number with every economic downturn.

The collapse of the East End shipbuilding in 1867 made the area synonymous with poverty. London was a city of small masters overwhelmingly involved in the finishing trades for consumer goods. Like work in the docks and the building trade, these sectors were affected by seasonal fluctuations in the demand for labour. It was common, for instance, for as many as one in three builders and the same fraction of dockers to find themselves laid off with the onset of winter. Many factory jobs also involved periods of idleness. In Lancashire's cotton industry periodic slumps meant that both spinners and weavers were often on 'short time' or laid off for weeks at a time. Such breaks in employment were the norm for most workers during the nineteenth century, which explains the great demand for jobs that offered steady employment, if only on mediocre pay, such as in breweries and on the railways.

Many of those in irregular employment, together with those who had lost steady employment, joined the great mass of those competing for casual jobs. To gain such jobs you needed neither a reference nor a recommendation. The lodging houses around the London Docks in the 1860s were typical of all those by Britain's quaysides, peopled by 'everything from decayed and bankrupt master butchers, publicans and grocers to old soldiers, discharged lawyer's clerks and thieves trying for work'. At that time there were about 20,000 people dependent on the docks for a livelihood. As reported by Mayhew, 'The courts and alleys around the docks are packed with low lodging houses. Those who live in the area, in addition to dockers, are sack-makers, watermen and that peculiar class of London poor who pick up a precarious living by the water side.' The latter were those who scoured the banks of the Thames for the detritus daily washed up on its banks, including timber and metal.

At the centre of this area were the parishes of St George, Shadwell and Wapping, some of the most overcrowded in the country with an average of seven people per house – which made them fifty per cent more crowded than those in the poorest part of Bethnal Green. In one of the largest lodging houses in this area, an investigator found in a 'small room on the ground floor between twenty and thirty of the most wretched objects I ever beheld. Some were shoeless, some coatless, others shirtless and from all these came so rank and foul a stench that I was sickened.'

These spectral figures were among those who constantly replenished the nation's enormous pool of casual labour. Whenever skilled men could find no employment in their own trade, whenever office workers were laid off in large numbers, whenever men lost their jobs on the land and flooded into the city, whenever immigrants landed on these shores, eager and hopeful, they invariably took their places among the dockers and market workers and increased the competition for casual work. For many of these people, the lodging house represented their first contact with a new, often alien environment and played a major part in inducting them into the mysteries of their new life.

In an age when cities were sucking in people from abroad and the surrounding countryside, the lodging house played a key role in helping people make the transition from rural, agricultural life to the rigours of the industrial city. For much of the nineteenth century it seemed the whole world was in transit, particularly in times of industrial growth and agricultural depression when the surplus rural population sought work in the cities. The vast majority of these newcomers rented a room or lodged either with a family or in a lodging house. Single men generally opted for lodging.

Evidence from the 1851 census for Leicester shows that one-fifth of all lodgers lived in groups of more than five; in other words, twenty per cent of all lodgers lived in what we would call a lodging house. In 1851 they made up twelve per cent of all households and five per cent of the population. In the poorest part of the city at least twenty per cent of households took in lodgers. This figure seems to be fairly typical of industrial towns in the second half of the nineteenth century: Preston's figure for 1851 was twenty-three per cent.

Figures from the 1881 census also show something else of interest: people wanted to lodge with their own countrymen. Thus, there was a significant tendency for the Irish to lodge in houses with a noticeable Irish element. In Liverpool, seventy-five per cent of Irish lodgers lived in households with Irish heads; in Huddersfield it was eighty per cent and eighty-seven per cent in Cardiff. The same trend applied to Germans, Italians and Jews. This strongly suggests that the lodging house was an important means by which newcomers adapted to the city. By lodging with their countrymen, they eased the transition and found familiarity and support when all around them was strange and challenging. In the days before the labour exchanges such contacts were an invaluable means of finding work, support and camaraderie.

Those dependent on employment that was precarious were not, of course, confined to the great centres of population. Though it was often implied that the frequenters of lodging houses in the market towns were chiefly peripatetic thieves, beggars and tramps, the evidence suggests otherwise. In fact, there were many long-term or semi-permanent lodgers and about a third of these were locally born.

Many were general labourers who sought work on a day-to-day basis, sometimes referred to as 'catch work' labourers. Not infrequently these people were middle-aged bachelors and many were farm labourers, walking to their work each day, often as far as four miles. Other common occupations among the frequent users of lodging houses were drovers and soldiers and about a third were women, the majority in the company of a male companion.

To the middle class, however, lodging houses posed a danger. For them, the family provided the best possible context for adapting to economic fluctuations and those whose lifestyle not only excluded family life but also, as in the case of those living in a lodging house, actually precluded it, were likely to fall prey to all the ills of rootlessness – poverty, immorality and lawlessness. It was also widely accepted that the family nurtured the ethics of economic success – encouraging providence and industry – and in times of crisis provided support and self-help. Yet there is no doubt that lodging houses reduced homelessness in the expanding industrial towns and ensured that poverty, often the result of irregular, casual employment, did not always consign people to the workhouse. Lodging houses of the smaller type were particularly beneficial to the newcomers, as these were frequently homes in which the owners lived with their family and provided lodgers with a share in that life.

There is no doubt that lodging houses helped craftsmen to adapt to the culture of their own trade. Many decent lodging houses catered for specific crafts. In 1851, for instance, the Boot public house in College Street, Northampton, housed coachbuilders from all over the British Isles, while the Lion & Lamb in Bridge Street housed many tailors. It was common for large-scale retailers employing many staff to accommodate them in dormitories, as was the experience of H.G. Wells, fictionalised in his novel *Kipps*.

As the century wore on, the number of skilled workers found in such places continued to dwindle. In the early days of trade unions they supplied their members with accommodation at lodges and pubs. Later they provided travelling allowances and then unemployed benefits. In this respect the position of skilled men was incomparably better than that of the unskilled, who were pushed back on their own resources.

For those unable to compete in this harsh world, there were limited alternatives. One was to join the army. For many, however, this proved no more than a deferment of the inevitable. Few soldiers leaving the army had acquired any new skills that might lift them above the mass of the unskilled. In fact, the minute pension with which most returned to civilian life was for many the seal that held them in the trap of casual labour for the rest of their days. The pension was always too little to live on and insufficient to make it possible to avoid work altogether. Chelsea pensioners, for instance, were commonly found in lodging houses. Serving soldiers – moving from one posting to another – were also a staple among the residents.

The condition of the lodging houses around the London Docks and those in every other major port tells us a great deal about their occupants. Mayhew visited one large lodging house near the docks, which it appeared to be an outhouse of some sort, the size of a barn, its walls unplastered and the roof shot through with holes, so that whenever it rained water poured through. A grimy table ran around one wall and provided support for a score of 'ragged, greasy wretches', while others huddled around the fire, toasting herrings, drying out cigar ends and boiling potatoes in a coffee pot.

Of the thirty men there, eight were occasional dockers, who managed at best to get three days' work a week. When out of work they lacked the 2*d* necessary for a bed and had to walk the streets all night. These men told Mayhew that it was common for them to go several days without food or drink and in winter they often went a fortnight or three weeks without a day's work.

Some of these men set off for Billingsgate Market where they hoped to earn a few pence as porters. Most were young, two-thirds under 21. As for the dormitory where they slept, it struck Mayhew as 'exactly the same as a Dissenting chapel, the divisions between the beds standing up like partitions between the pews. Stretched there like corpses, in a bed as narrow as a coffin' were many shirtless men with only a rug or a leather sheet as a cover.

Later Mayhew ventured back to the same area on a Sunday to find all the shops open and the streets thronging with prostitutes and sailors. Standing about in languid circles were clusters of Irish labourers, smoking short pipes amid washing lines 'dangling dirty white clothes to dry' while 'ragged, unwashed, shoeless children scampered past'. In doorways, huddled and shivering, slept a number of prostitutes. In the lodging houses he visited, which he believed were typical, he saw no one eating with cutlery, only their hands.

One particular house was home to sixty people, of whom about half were pickpockets, ten street beggars, some old and infirm who lived on charity or relief, ten to fifteen dockers and the same number of labourers in 'low and precarious callings', but also a few 'reduced from good circumstances'. At one stage there were nine people who made a living by collecting dog dung – used in the manufacture of leather and known in the trade as 'the pure' – for which they received 5*s* a basketful. Additionally, the house was usually home to several 'bone-grubbers' who made a living out of things they found discarded in the streets – everything from bones and rags to pieces of metal. By this means they managed to scratch an income of about a shilling a day. Similarly, a number of mud larks manage to subsist on what they found washed up on the banks of the Thames.

Jack London, another student of the underclass, was struck most of all by the sense of deadening hopelessness which these lodging houses embodied. Watching men eating in silence, he sensed 'a feeling of gloom pervading the ill-lighted place' making him wonder 'what evil they had done that they should be punished so'. He divided those he encountered into two categories, which he called the young and hilarious and the old and gloomy.

Wandering, London soon came to realise, was no life for an old man. In the intense competition of the nomadic life, the old invariably went under. It became increasingly common for houses to compel lodgers to leave in the morning. Consequently old, unemployable men had to carry all their possessions with them while they trudged the streets. Many of these impoverished, elderly people became so dispirited that they drifted towards the workhouse and resigned themselves to the indignity of 'going on the parish' or sought accommodation offered by charitable institutions such as the Salvation Army.

For most, however, this was unconscionable. Yet commentators were unanimous in their conviction that the lodging house was no place for those of 'needy respectability'. The model lodging house, they were convinced, was the antidote to the evils of the common lodging house.

The Panacea: The Model Lodging House

The earliest products of philanthropy, such as those established by the Peabody Trust, provided accommodation for families and made no provision for single men. This came later with those models designed to provide clean and orderly surroundings in a wholesome atmosphere, which would allow the poor to escape the degradation of squalor while at the same time offering the institution's shareholders a fair return on their investment. In addition it was anticipated that they would set standards which other strictly commercial lodging houses would be required to meet, if they were to compete, and also raise the expectations and aspirations of the poor.

The prototype of the model lodging house, the Destitute Sailors' Asylum, appeared in 1835 and was opened for the benefit of seamen. The project of naval officer Captain R.J. Elliott and funded though the financial support of the Queen Dowager, Adelaide, the wife of William IV, the house was designed by Henry Roberts. It stood on Well Street, by the London Docks, where it accommodated 300.

Roberts was also responsible for other models in London as well as Tunbridge Wells and Windsor. Later mendacity houses sprang up in Banbury, Oxford, Cambridge and other places, offering a single night's accommodation to those who agreed to leave the area the following day. The Albert Street, Mile End, lodging house, built by the Metropolitan Association for Improving the Dwellings of the Industrious Classes, accommodated 110 families and was full from the day it opened in 1848. The Association's building in Albert Street, Spitalfields, accommodated 60 families and made provision for 234 single men. Surrounded by open spaces, it included baths and wash-houses and all 'requisite appurtenances' – a reading room, a coffee room, workshops, a kitchen and facilities for buying drinks. Each sleeping compartment had its own window for light and ventilation and each lodger had his own key. State of the art washrooms and lavatories were plentiful. When it opened in 1849 the cost was 3s a week for a single man.

A *Times* editorial of the day described the Spitalfield's House as 'so clean, so airy, so wholesome and altogether so inviting that one almost longs to live in it one's self and make use of its endless accommodations'. The benefits were, the author believed, not merely physical: 'It is a good and improving thing to be quiet, domestic, methodical and clean; to live by rule; and above all to pay one's rent punctually at the stipulated time.' Its tenants were weekly tenants and therefore it was no place for the itinerant worker.

The Association was convinced that it was not only its tenants who benefitted from its provision: they were forcing other landlords to improve their properties in order to compete. Landlords who failed to improve would be wiped out for 'who but the most depraved would not prefer a light, dry, clean and wholesome abode to a dark, damp cellar, when he can have the one on the same terms as the other?'

However, John Holllingshead was only one of many contemporaries who felt that such places were largely a waste of money, in that they helped only those who were,

> well able to help themselves. The main beneficiaries are people who have no genuine entitlement to the largesse of this sort of philanthropy. The costermongers, the street hawkers, the industrious poor are still rotting on their filthy, ill-drained, ill-ventilated courts, while well-paid mechanics, porters and clerks, willing to sacrifice a certain portion of their self-respect, are the constant tenants of these model dwellings.

He goes on to analyse the occupants of model housing built in Bethnal Green by Angela Burdett Coutts. Rents there were beyond the means of the poorest at as much as 4*s* per week. Weavers at the time earned about 7*s* a week and to spend up to 60 per cent of that on accommodation was beyond their means.

Only six of the fifty lodgers in the models Holllingshead studied were locals and all were 'a little more advanced in cleanliness and civilization and quick to see where 10/- of comfort is selling for less than half price'. In 1860 there were over 6,000 tenants in model lodging houses. Hollingshead recounts a visit to one in Charles Street, Drury Lane, designed to hold eighty-two men each at 4*d* a night or 2*s* for the week. 'In the kitchen about a dozen men were standing about … some cooking at the fire, others talking and idling. One old man was writing and another asleep with his head and arms lying among some broken potatoes on the table. They looked all greasy, faded men, men difficult to keep clean, who smelt of onions.' Many were lawyers' clerks, linen drapers' assistants and mechanics. 'Some stopped for years, some a month and some only a night.'

Hollingshead remained convinced that these places did nothing for what he called 'the lowest of the low', partly because the third of the population who live in London squalor 'have little demand for pure, wholesome, well-constructed dwellings'. They are inured to their conditions and 'aspire to nothing more'. In effect, these places were of no benefit to those for whom they were designed and instead developed into a charity for skilled workers and the lower middle classes. An account of a model in Charles Street in 1861 seems to confirm this as one observer recounts 'the land-lady, an old lady who regarded herself as the mother of them all, told me that many [of the lodgers] were lawyer's clerks, linen drapers' assistants and mechanics … she had never had but one costermonger – a most superior man of his kind, who lived there for two years until he got married when he left.'

Rowton Houses, the work of the Tory peer Lord Rowton, were the largest and most innovative of London's model lodging houses. The success of the Vauxhall house was such that this 'hotel for the working man' became the standard by which all other models were judged. A further five were built on the same lines at King's Cross, Hammersmith, Whitechapel, Camden and Newington Butts. The press was fulsome in its praise of the facilities provided for single men, each with his own sleeping cubicle, ventilated with a window, and communal facilities including a day room and gardens. The entrance was deliberately imposing, causing one visitor to exclaim that the place was nothing less than 'a palace for working men'.

Rowton paid great attention to the layout of the accommodation and there is no doubt that it far exceeded anything previously available to working men. Critics likened the houses to the West End clubs frequented by the upper class and lauded his attempts to introduce lodgers to a 'shared domesticity' of the sort regarded as central to stable family life. The first thing the visitor saw – enormous doors of polished teak – could not fail to impress. The entrance hall was well lit, glazed and decorated with plants to create the feeling of a substantial hotel.

Lodgers had to present themselves before 7pm and were allocated a cubicle. Additionally, they had use of day rooms, the kitchen, libraries, the smoke room and repair rooms where they could tend to worn clothes and distressed boots. Glazed brick and tiled interiors made it easy to keep clean. Decorations consisted largely of etchings and paintings, many based on those displayed in the Houses of Parliament, and stags' heads of the type found in the homes of the aristocracy. Together with the range of amenities available, these features contributed to an aura of domesticity far removed from the sterile institutional atmosphere of the workhouse or the harsh functionality of the common lodging house.

However, at 6*d* a night they were beyond the means of the poorest. In fact the 1901 census reveals that lodgers were of a surprisingly diverse nature and were virtually all gainfully employed. Many were working men but there were a surprising number of clerks, shop assistants, accountants and lowly estate agents. The premises had to be vacated during the day but this was no hardship for those in work, and though payment was by the day it was possible to become a semi-permanent resident by renewing day after day and week after week. Lodgers shared not only the facilities but frequently chores such as washing and cooking.

Nevertheless, it is wrong to assume that the atmosphere was that of an enclosed religious order – there were plenty of drunken and noisy men at weekends and there is evidence of illicit sexual activity. Nor were lodgers invariably honest: complaints of petty theft were common. The privacy provided by the cubicles was only partial, in that there was a large gap between the top of the partition and the ceiling which failed to keep out noise. Yet, there were a number of courtyards, some on the rooftop, with benches available for recreation and leisure. All in all they were places of comfortable order.

A similar institution, Victoria House, once stood at the junction of Commercial Road and Wentworth Street and dominated the area off Whitechapel Road. A converted warehouse, it had a distinctive character different from Rowton House: it was patently religious and consciously spartan. Inmates had to embrace temperance – or at least tolerate it while staying there. Its most striking feature was the enormous lecture halls where preachers sought to transform the outlook of lodgers.

St Giles was once one of the most feared rookeries in London. In an attempt to tackle the lack of decent accommodation there, the Society for the Improvement of the Working Classes built what is now Parnell House in 1849. The Society built another house in the Seven Dials, towards Covent Garden, where the vegetable market and the theatre districts ran up against each other. This area was for much of the nineteenth century notorious for prostitution and the squalor of its lodging houses. In the mid-century the Famine Irish flooded into the area. Charles Street Model Lodging House stood in Mecklin Street (formerly Charles Street) and held about eighty. The original building, erected in 1847, was refurbished and renamed Shaftsbury Chambers in 1892.

It was in the same area that London County Council (LCC) made its first contribution to housing the poor. Parker House, on Parker Street, opened in 1896 with provision for hundreds of men, while a few streets away the enormous Bruce House, on Kemble Street, built in 1895, in addition to beds for over 1,000 single men, offered dayrooms, a shop, a barber, a tailor and a boot mender – in fact everything the itinerant worker could want. Ashley Chambers, at nearby Wild Court, was another LCC house. The accommodation in all these houses far exceeded what was available elsewhere at 6*d* a night. Once more the newspapers likened their facilities to a gentleman's club.

As for the nature of the lodgers, we have a detailed picture of what the 220 lodgers in Bruce House, on Kemble Street, Drury Lane did for a living around the beginning of the twentieth century. There were thirty-five who addressed circulars, a common form of domestic labour by which people eked out a bare subsistence. A further thirty-three were labourers and street or market hawkers. Some, with disarming candour, described themselves as beggars. This is much as one might expect. However, surprisingly there were also two school teachers, two insurance agents, three engineers, nine clerks and five described poetically as 'broken down gentlemen'; then, as now, the social ladder did not convey people only in one direction. To leaven the mix there was also a doctor, an actor, a solicitor and a framer. Several of these regarded the house as their home and occupied the same cubicle for years.

A hostel erected by the Society for the Improvement of the Condition of the Labouring Classes stood in George Street, Bloomsbury, and provided accommodation for 104 single men. It comprised a kitchen, a wash-house, baths with hot and cold water, a pantry and 'a secure and separate well-ventilated safe for the food of each inmate', a library, a common room – decorated with white tiles on brick arches – with two rows of elm tables and seats, a fireplace and a constant supply of hot water. There were eight dormitories, 'subdivided with moveable wooden partitions 6' 9" high, each with its own door within which is a well ventilated area with a bed, chair, clothes box, gaslight and heating as required. There are washing closets on each floor.' Unsurprisingly, people flocked there in far greater numbers than could be accommodated. Their charges were similar to those of landlords offering infinitely inferior provision.

The Society for Improving the Condition of the Labouring Classes went on to build an entire street of workers' houses on Streatham Street, Bloomsbury, designed to 'combine every point essential to the health, comfort and moral habits of inmates; particularly with respect to ventilation, drainage and an ample supply of water'. When they opened in 1846 the rent for the most basic family accommodation was from 3*s* to 6*s* a week. The Society's President, Prince Albert, also erected a block of model houses at Cavalry Barracks in Hyde Park entirely at his own expense. These were designed by the Prince and exhibited at the Great

Exhibition of 1851. The initial hope and expectation was that these efforts would show that it was possible to make a fair return on investment in cheap accommodation and therefore capitalists, whose philanthropic instincts were tempered by hard-headed business calculation, would fill the breach left by philanthropy. But rising land prices in the 1850s meant that the return on such an investment was insufficient to tempt the shrewd entrepreneur.

To be viable, models required a large population of tenants to ensure they operated at full capacity. Consequently the bulk of them were in London, though there were some in other centres of population. The Bradford Model Lodging House Company Limited opened a house in the city in 1866. This philanthropic enterprise was designed to provide investors with an annual return of 5 per cent. It accommodated almost 60,000 people over a 12 month period, during which time more than 5,000 were turned away for lack of room.

Despite their many qualities, there remained many who agreed with Hollingshead in questioning the benefits of such enterprises. Thomas Archer bemoaned the fact that 'half a million of money … for providing improved dwellings for the poor should be used for the purpose of adding to the convenience of the comparatively well-to-do'. He too stressed that model lodging houses did nothing to help those at the bottom of the economic pile.

Additionally, the rules in the models were not to the liking of certain elements of the working class. This was most evident in the Peabody buildings, where rents had to be paid in advance, arrears were not allowed, and all applications required an employer's reference. This meant that casual workers were effectively barred, as were most types of home workers who were not allowed to carry on their trade on Peabody premises. Peabody buildings also provided very few units for single people and these were often reserved for the aged, widows and widowers.

It is important to put the models in context. They had a minor impact on the lodging population as there was so little of this type of accommodation; the number of Londoners occupying them in the nineteenth century was equivalent to half the capital's annual population growth. Archer also claims that 'these places have something of the institutional censure of the workhouse about them that deters many for the poorer classes prefer a place where they can go in and out without it being anybody's business'.

Archer suggested that life in such places drained the spirit of a man and led to depression:

> Despite all its acknowledged advantages, men are driven from the place after a few weeks by sheer ennui, almost by a kind of reasonless aversion to its regularity and completeness and above all by want of personality about the building and its arrangements. They drift into some place in the neighbourhood – many degrees dirtier, less comfortable and less reputable than the place from which they have pined to be free. These places destroy all individuality and self-respect as they exude an institutional reek.

Confirmation of this comes from experience of one Rowton House which serves its original function to the present day: Arlington House in Camden Town. In the early 1930s Orwell wrote of it in *Down and Out in Paris and London*, where he praised it as superb value for money, at a time when 1s bought a cubicle and for 2s 6d a 'special' was to be had, 'which is practically hotel accommodation'. Orwell, however, found the strict discipline irksome. It seems that the rules posted on the walls prohibited most things, including card playing and cooking.

Other benefactors for whom housing became the focus of their philanthropic efforts varied greatly in their resources. The East End vicar, the Reverend Barnett, founded the East London Dwelling Company to buy and refurbish properties to provide decent housing for the poor. By 1886 he had established Brunswick Buildings and Wentworth Buildings right in the heart of the Spitalfields rookery. Their success attracted, among other philanthropists, the Rothschilds, whose Four Per Cent Dwellings Company erected Rothschild House, home to 200 Jewish families. Accommodation was basic and the building was like a military barracks. In common with most other philanthropic housing projects, it attracted criticism for not helping those at the bottom of the social hierarchy – particularly the geriatric destitute and the chronically sick. Only the industrious and provident poor could afford the rent and the 1885 Commission on the Housing of the Working Classes found that most of the families occupying this sort of accommodation were those of respectable artisans or those with more than a single income.

Father Arthur Osborne Jay opened the Trinity Chambers Lodging House in the Nichol at the end of the nineteenth century. He offered beds at 2s a week – below the market rate – and refused to take tramps. His ninety-two lodgers enjoyed hot baths, the use of a kitchen and a common room. He had no illusions about the prospects of his clients if they remained in Britain and encouraged them to emigrate to Canada and Australia.

With the 1851 Labouring Classes Lodging House Act the government first became involved in the provision of accommodation and sought to make up for the deficiencies of philanthropic efforts. The Act allowed local authorities to buy, lease or build lodging houses. It laid down detailed instructions on how they should set their charges: not so high as to exclude the working man in search of employment but not so low as to be an indirect form of poor relief.

Most local authorities, however, were reluctant to undertake the burden of Westminster's munificence, towards which Parliament intended to make no practical contribution. They were under no compulsion to do so as the powers conferred by the Act were optional. Local councils realised from the outset that municipal accommodation would never – because of the nature of its clientele – be self-financing. Significantly, they also realised that if municipal lodging houses were to become indiscriminate charities they would attract professional scroungers and ne'er-do-wells in great numbers.

By the time beds in models became available in large numbers they cost between 2s and 3s a week, that is almost twice the price of the average common lodging house. One effect of this was that few of them were ever full. Most councils took the view that rather than building lodging houses they would do better to improve existing ones. Consequently models remained very much the domain of philanthropy, with a few exceptions.

Besides, models were not viable outside the centres of population and had little impact elsewhere. Outside the great cities, in the countless villages and market towns across Britain, there was also an enormous population constantly in motion in addition to large numbers for whom the lodging house was a settled home.

Chapter Five

Harvesters, Hucksters and Harpists: The Common Lodging House in the County Towns

According to Philip Larkin, the substance of a man's life consists of a succession of small indignities, things known only to himself. Most of us become inured to minor humiliations and do not despise ourselves when we laugh fulsomely at the boss's jokes. Others feel the sting of every insult. One such individual was a street clown, interviewed by a social commentator in the 1850s.

'You can't imagine what a curse the street business often becomes,' he said, 'with its insults and starvations. I dare say that no persons think more of their dignity than persons in my way of life.' Expressing a sentiment common among the people of the street, he said he would 'rather starve than ask for relief from the parish. Many times I've gone to work without a breakfast and played the clown until I could raise a dinner. Most of the street clowns,' he added 'die in the workhouse. In their old age they are generally very wretched and poverty-stricken.' His garish attire of red and white stripes, spattered with red and black spots, belied his despair.

The clown's life, grim as it was, would have been even worse had it not been for the network of lodging houses which by the mid-nineteenth century criss-crossed Britain. Without them neither he nor any of the itinerant army of entertainers and hawkers would have been able to ply their trade. These were the people who gave the streets their distinctive character. Fiddles and trombones, organs and drums, voices baritone and bass filled the air. It was impossible for the Victorian to venture into the street without encountering some delight which attracted an audience of children and street Arabs eager for distraction.

Most of these performers were itinerants, smitten by wanderlust, forever searching for audiences more appreciative and more generous. In large cities the range of distractions seen over the course of a year included every form of musicianship, every conceivable act of agility and every imaginable entertainment. This great entertainment fraternity, in common with itinerant peddlers, wintered in the big cities and began to circulate around the country in April, moving from one lodging house to another, brightening the lives of all they encountered.

There were an enormous number of these people in the 1800s and their numbers increased in the second half of the century. In 1891 there were over 7,000 actors, 39,000 musicians and 9,000 'performers and showmen'. There were numerous touring theatrical companies and few county towns in which German bands did not perform at least once during the summer months. In 1891 there were over 1,200 German musicians, most of whom were constantly on the move. Such bands visited Banbury every spring for over forty years.

There were even more Italian musicians, many of whom travelled alone or in pairs and reached most villages and towns in even the remotest parts of the country. There were also Irish musicians – fiddlers and pipers, accordion and bodhrán players. These however, were a mere fraction of the number of native musicians – everything from 'professors of music' to clog dancers and the blind or disabled fiddlers. All used the lodging houses.

The street singer was generally known as a 'griddler'. 'Chanters' were those who sang the broadsheet songs they peddled. One of the commonest street entertainers was the ballad-singer. His ingenuity lay in telling of dramatic news items – gruesome murders, executions and bloody wars made excellent subject matter – in the form of a ballad which he would sing in order to promote the sale of their ballad sheets, printed on long sheets of paper and often displayed on a clotheshorse. The sheets sold for a penny or a halfpenny. 'Praters', who sang hymns and religious songs, were to be seen and heard in virtually every city and town in the country.

In addition there were Christy Minstrels, animal trainers – though the beast they had tamed might be nothing more ferocious than a poodle coached to stand on its hind legs – and jugglers. It is a measure of how many street entertainers there were that in the 1860s Michael Bass MP led a campaign to suppress them. The chief effect of this, despite the Act he piloted through Parliament in 1864, was to make Mr Bass and those who supported him immensely unpopular with the poor who denounced them as curmudgeonly killjoys.

Some of the most interesting entertainers were those seen only at specific times of the year. Jack in the Green, a character whose origins go back to pagan antiquity, appeared on May Day, also known as Chimney Sweep's Day. The sweep, his wife and family took to the streets. Encased from head to foot in a wicker frame not unlike a beehive, with boughs and flowers woven into it and only a small window to see through, the sweep was entirely concealed. His family, their faces blackened with soot and the women in short white dresses and gaudy shoes, played mouth organs around the dancing sweep and collected coppers from the crowd.

Puppet shows, then as now, exercised an unrivalled fascination for children. The puppeteer was generally accompanied by a helper in a white top hat, playing a mouth organ and often a drum. It was his role to collect the donations at the end of the show.

In November Guy Fawkes appeared in an array of elaborately demonic forms, sometimes drawn on a cart and often accompanied by exotically dressed figures who played instruments and worked the crowd.

Similar to the street clowns were the street dancers, from old soldiers, who bemoaned the fact that they might 'dance half an hour for a ha'penny', to faux ballerinas. One unfortunate soldier wore an artillery man's blue jacket, grey trousers and a dark blue army cap. Yet he confided in Mayhew that he lived in a lodging house of the better kind, which admitted only adults. Cryptically, he added: 'I couldn't bear to live in a house where there were boys and girls, and all sorts – there's such carryings on.'

Animal shows of staggering ingenuity exercised an irresistible pull on the Victorian public. One of the most intriguing was 'Happy Family' in which the showman displayed an enormous wire cage on the back of a cart or a wheelbarrow which housed a dog, a cat, half a dozen mice, canaries, finches and sometimes a small monkey, all co-existing in perfect harmony. The trainer opened the cage door and called the cats by the names of famous boxers at which they sprang onto their hind legs, walked out onto a miniature stage and, donning boxing gloves on their forepaws, bobbed and weaved while delivering upper-cuts and kidney punches. Next the dog responded to questions by barking before emerging from the cage and breaking up the cats' fight.

Conjurers, jugglers and magicians always drew large crowds, while musicians were so common that they found it hard to attract an audience. The hoarse wail of the Tyrolean pipes – invariably accompanied by white mice, marmots or a squirrel in a rotating cage – filled the air of many a Victorian street, usually playing twelve bars of the same tune incessantly and the fairground whirr of the hurdy-girdy was as common as the clip-clop of horses' hooves.

Organ grinders elicited a powerful reaction. They gave children and street Arabs a focal point and enlivened the day for many. Small organs were of two types. The soprano of the type was the tall-backed tinkling instrument that gave little offence, while the thundering bass was a wind and reed contraption in a rectangular casing which produced a deep and full sound. In both cases the musician carried his instrument on his back and, when playing, supported it on folding legs. The casing often doubled as a stage for a dancing monkey, with pillbox hat and a maroon waistcoat with gold piping.

Far less common was the 'marrow-bone and cleaver band', who used large animal bones like castanets to strike the sharp edge of a meat cleaver. By this means they produced a powerful rhythm without any tune as they usually accompanied a butcher's wedding. Bells were also popular and usually set out on a wooden frame. In order to gain a competitive edge some musicians introduced a novelty element – in one case in the form of a dun mare that played 'Home Sweet Home' by striking the bells with her right hoof.

Musicians, genuinely and professionally blind, formed a sub-class of those who exploited their misfortune as much as their musical prowess. As in every area of streetcraft, success was enhanced by a novelty dimension. At least one blind musician played a violin with his feet while playing another in the conventional manner. Other fiddlers specialised in using their instrument to recreate the sounds of the farmyard, producing the bellow of a bull, the lowing of a calf, the bark of a dog, the crowing of a cock, the cluck of a hen and the screech of a peacock. Buskers' dexterity was always amusing and those who played six instruments were not uncommon. The busker was a common sight on Victorian streets and popular, though he often supplemented his income by selling obscene songs and occasionally performing in pubs, usually for free drink.

Street photographers erected their canvas booths on open ground near a busy thoroughfare. They invariably worked with a caller who advertised their services, calling 'Hi! Hi! Walk insides. Walk inside. Have your true likeness took, frame and glass complete and only sixpence!'

Street patterers chanted details of the murders recounted in the newspapers and periodicals they were selling. Many a reader complained that the enticing titbits which had induced them to buy the journal bore no relation to anything within its pages.

Deception was a complaint seldom made against the numerous hawkers and peddlers who circulated through the villages and towns of Victorian Britain, bringing goods to many who had no other access to them. These too depended on the lodging house for their way of life.

It is difficult for us to appreciate the enormous number of nineteenth century people who squeezed a living of sorts from street selling. Mayhew estimated that it formed the means by which 30,000 adults and an inestimable number of children survived in London alone in the 1840s and 1850s and he estimated that between 1 and 2 out of every 150 people sustained themselves by this method. There is no doubt that there were tens of thousands of others throughout the country who plied the same trades and many of these were itinerant. Their average income was generally no more than mere subsistence and fluctuated throughout the year, usually better in summer than in winter when it was often negligible.

The 1851 census shows that street sellers outnumbered general shopkeepers by about 30,000. There were another 8,000 who were categorised as 'General Dealers, Hucksters, Dealers in Small Wares and Costermongers', many of whom were probably indistinguishable from hawkers. They were to be found in over half the country's lodging houses in the mid-century and their numbers continued to grow until the 1870s. A high proportion were Irish.

The array of goods they sold included fabrics, linen, lace, buttons, tapes, pins, flowers and matches. The making and selling of knitted caps was common among lodgers. Many sold fruit and vegetables – often bought as surplus stock from local greengrocers – while the poorest sold cress. Sweets and confectionery were commonly sold, especially in areas where sugar production was based, including Daventry, Hereford, Kettering, Leicester, Lincoln, Northampton and Stamford. There were few market towns where muffins could not be had from street vendors, while herbal medicines and medical advice from doctors of dubious qualifications were freely available. For those with poor eyesight there was always a peddler offering a range of spectacles. Stationery of all sorts was sold by others who followed the wandering life, alongside the wares touted by makers of pin cushions, combs, mops and rat and bird catchers.

Some commodities, though apparently unsuitable for sale by hawkers, were nevertheless widely sold by them. Thus, careful hawkers dealt in crockery while those with broad backs and well developed biceps sold hardware and whetstones, fire shovels and dustpans and tinkers, tinmen, tinplate workers and braziers also dealt in the sale and repair of metal objects. There were many wireworkers who went from one lodging house to another as itinerant tradesmen. Basket-makers, sellers of mats and brushes, and men who hawked toys and jewellery all added to the variety of goods and services available.

Makers and repairers of umbrellas formed a large group and were to be found in almost every lodging house. Umbrellas with whale spokes were common and far too valuable to be simply discarded when broken. Match-sellers were among the poorest of the street vendors and were generally children or disabled adults who relied on the sympathy of customers. Some exchanged their wares – such as 'donkey stones' for cleaning doorsteps – for old clothes, while others specialised in clothing that was beginning to show signs of wear, going from door to door in middle-class areas buying such distressed garments. There was always a ready market for second-hand clothes: the majority of working class people never knew what it was to wear something that was not moulded to the contours of someone else's body.

There is little that the modern eco-warrior could tell our Victorian predecessors about recycling: they reused everything and were loath to waste anything. Much of the recycling of goods and materials that seemed beyond use depended on the residents of lodging houses. Clothes dealers, rag collectors and rag and bone men were fixtures in lodging houses. Marine stores employed lodgers from local lodging houses to gather virtually anything – broken furniture, threadbare garments, gaping shoes, discoloured dripping, skins, iron blistered with rust, rags, ashes from a thousand grates, bottles and even waste paper.

Hawkers and tinkers made up seventeen per cent of women lodgers and were the largest group among them. The reports of the Leicester Domestic Mission for the 1850s describe the lodging houses on the northern edge of the St Margaret's parish in South Wharf Street. No less than 40,000 people passed through this area's 38 lodging houses each year, a figure that rose during the following two decades when rapid industrialisation increased the city's demand for labour. Among the lodgers of the 1850s, peddlers, hawkers and general dealers, travellers in cloth and watercress-sellers made up the bulk of those who stayed for short periods. Nationally they accounted for more than half of lodgers in 1861 and in market towns, such as Oxford, they made up seventy per cent.

While hawkers and collectors were transient residents, it is clear that the lodging houses of many market towns were the semi-permanent homes to many agricultural labourers who travelled as far as six miles a day to and from work. Agricultural labourers were found in almost half the country's lodging houses in 1861, and in greatest numbers within those counties with large estates which employed many labourers, such as Lincolnshire. Single men and widowers were in the majority and in areas where the gang system operated they were also found in large numbers.

Many houses provided accommodation for particular types of agricultural labourers. In 1851 the Mitre in Corve Street, Ludlow, was kept by Robert Allum, a drillman, whose house was favoured by other drillmen. The same clustering in specific lodging houses is found among drain-diggers, timber fellers and travelling clog-makers.

The Irish featured prominently among agricultural labourers, especially among seasonal workers. Describing Leicester's lodging houses in the 1850s, Joseph Dare noted that many of their occupants were Irish, 'who crowded in particularly at harvest time'. Speaking of the summer of 1847, he recorded that a two-room house, normally occupied by an Irishman, his wife and six children, accommodated an additional fourteen harvesters. There was at that time no supervision of lodging houses and Dare was by no means alone in calling for regulation, particularly necessary because of the dangers posed by 'the lower classes of dwelling, the abodes of the newly-arrived Irish'.

In the first half of the nineteenth century Irish men provided most of the additional labour needed at harvest time. Every year they crossed the Irish Sea and moved from one harvesting area to another – from hop fields to corn, from vegetables to potatoes. As the century progressed hops became the preserve of Londoners, above all East Enders.

Navvies were famed for constructing their own, often lawless encampments. The evidence, however, suggests that many of those working on major engineering projects near towns and villages used inns and lodging houses. This is certainly true of the Severn Valley Railway construction in 1861. In the same year railway construction provided employment for almost 40,000 men and navvies were to be found in nearly every lodging house throughout the country.

Whereas navvies working in cities always had a choice of lodging houses, small towns often had only one. Regardless of its location, according to W.H. Davies, the renowned tramp, navvies were never comfortable in lodging houses as they were the object of the contempt of both peddlers and beggars, who regarded them as mugs for having to work for a living. But for those travelling in search of work they were the only alternative to the casual wards of the workhouse, many of which were small and often full at certain times of year. In addition, working men, in common with beggars, objected to them on the grounds that they were demeaning.

Market town lodging houses averaged less than ten occupants, though it is sometimes difficult to determine the exact number of lodgers in the smaller houses; the household often included the keeper's family and live-in servants and the distinction between these is not always clear. As in the industrial cities and towns, market town lodging houses were frequently clustered in particular streets. In Oxford, for instance, St Thomas's High Street was the nucleus of over twenty lodging houses, where a bed was to be had for as little as 2*d* a night. In Banbury they centred on Ragrow, Wantage and Grove Street.

Some were substantial buildings, originally prestigious homes in areas that had gone to seed, roughly converted for multiple occupancy, with the emphasis on cramming in as many paying customers as was humanly possible, with little regard for the requirements of hygiene, health, decency or good order. Some lodgers slept in cellars. In rural areas it was common for the owner and his family to share the house. An analysis of the residents of Oxford lodging houses shows that almost half were men under 45 with only about a sixth older men and the same fraction children. A surprising number – one in four – were women, who were usually married, whereas most of the men were single.

Though there were lodgers from all over the country most were local. At every stage of the nineteenth century the Irish were found in many houses, their numbers peaking during the Famine, from 1845–50. Though the array of lodgers' occupations was considerable, they were chiefly unskilled labourers: crossing sweepers, hawkers, street entertainers, abandoned women, labourers, domestics, match-sellers, agricultural and railway workers, travelling fair workers and the ubiquitous tramping navvy. Many were in seasonal employment and the majority were transients, though there were some permanent and semi-permanent lodgers.

All those who worked in the transport industry including drovers and cattle dealers, carters and waggoners, together with the crews of barges and narrow boats, used the lodging houses situated along trade routes. Sailors, both genuine and of the turnpike variety, also used them en route to and from their vessels.

'Crimps' – those who preyed on sailors – were thick on the ground in all major ports and particularly along the Thames. Theoretically these predators were owners of lodging houses, used by sailors, but in reality this was no more than a pretext for their chief source of income. Generally, the more professional crimps boarded ships making their way up the Thames at Gravesend and latched onto sailors looking for lodgings. They took sailors' belongings to their lodging house and, as mariners frequently had to wait for their wages after reaching port, lent them money at exorbitant interest rates. They also directed their prey to particular prostitutes. Before his leave was over the sailor owed money to the crimp and was often forced to get into further debt to acquire the things he needed to go to sea again – which the crimp supplied at inflated prices.

Similarly, there were few nineteenth century soldiers unfamiliar with lodging houses as they were often used by soldiers in transit and recruiting parties. There were almost 300,000 soldiers in the British army in 1861; almost 40 per cent were Irish-born and 10 per cent Scots. Most regiments, of course, had links with specific shires. Old soldiers were also a standard part of lodging house life and Chelsea pensioners were to be found in many, even outside London.

Though unskilled labourers made up the bulk of lodgers in the market towns, skilled men were also to be found, especially in the first sixty years of the century when many travelled in search of employment. It was not until the second half of the nineteenth century that factory production of most consumer goods became the norm. Prior to that most craftsmen were subject to seasonal fluctuation in demand for their labour, which left them with no alternative but to travel in search of work.

These were the 'tramping artisans' including marble polishers, cabinet-makers, tailors, shoe-makers, masons, carpenters, basket and box-makers, wireworkers, iron founders, umbrella and furniture repairers. Many of these were frequently found in lodging houses and a number of them were semi-permanent residents, but some also used the tramp wards. Before the age of labour exchanges even skilled men had to go looking for work. Add to this the short- and long-term trade cycles which forced people to move in search of employment and the vagaries of war, which sent soldiers and sailors scurrying from one end of the country to the other, and it is easy to see that then, as now, Britain was a realm in constant movement.

London shoe-makers, cabinet-makers and those in the clothing trade worked towards peaks of demand in March and October. In the university towns of Oxford and Cambridge demand was at its greatest during term time, in Leicestershire during the hunting season and in times of big meetings in towns near race courses. Building workers were in the same situation, but so also were servants, grooms, footmen and all those in domestic service. Couriers, foundry workers, coach and carriage-makers, French polishers, printers and cork cutters were merely a fraction of those who spent a large part of their lives chasing work. A study of the 1861 census for market towns shows that skilled men were found in six out of every ten lodging houses.

Nail-makers were in a similar situation. Though concentrated in the Black Country and Derbyshire, 'travelling nailers' were to be found in lodging houses all over the country, as were hawkers of clay tobacco pipes.

The quality of accommodation available in market towns, like that in the centres of population, varied greatly. Chester's lodging houses are described in a report of 1845, which has little good to say of them. They were apparently 'very miserable and wretched', many without bedsteads or even beds, with lodgers huddling together on straw instead. The rooms were often overcrowded and there was seldom any ventilation.

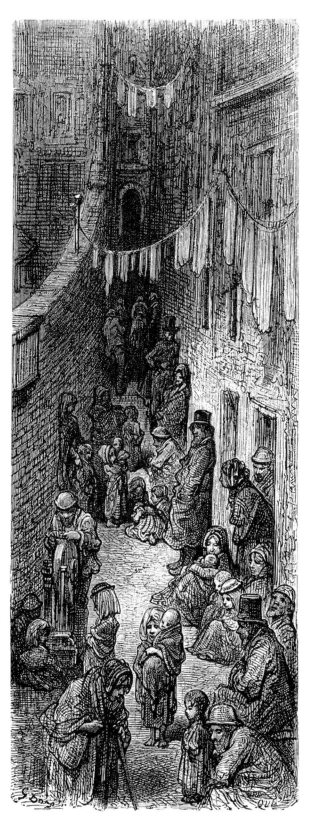

Orange Court, Drury Lane, was typical of the slums in which many of the worst lodging houses were located. *(Author's own collection)*

(Above) Dorset Street, at the heart of the area where the Ripper's victims lived. *(Right)* A lodging house in Flower and Dean Street, 'the foulest and most dangerous street in the metropolis'. (*Spitalfields Life*)

Cheap lodging houses such as this one located in the London docklands, pictured in the 1860s, were invaluable to those in precarious employment. *(Author's own collection)*

The kitchen was the centre of the lodging house in more raucous establishments. *(Author's own collection)*

Some lodging houses were a little more sedate than others. (*Spitalsfields Life*)

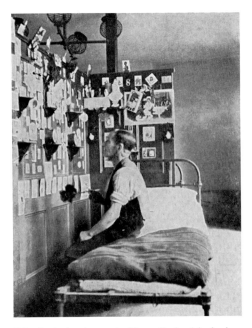

John Jay's dosshouse in Shoreditch. (*Author's own collection*)

One of the numerous cheap doss houses in the East End advertising beds for four pence a night. (Jack London, *People of the Abyss* (London: Inster & Co, 1903). *With thanks to Simon Fowler*)

This picture of the Manchester Ship Canal makes clear the enormous amount of physical labour required to carry out the great engineering feats of the nineteenth century. (*Mark Fynn Postcards*)

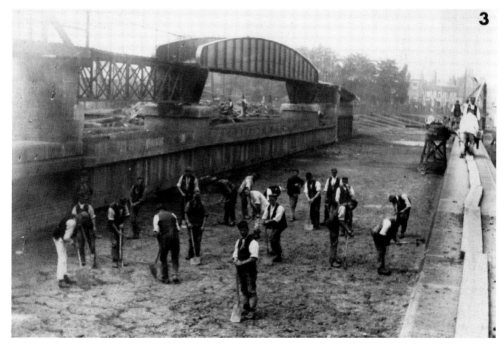

Men at Puddle on the Barton Aqueduct, demonstrating that every stage of construction of the Canal was labour intensive. (*Mullineux Collection, Chetham's Library*)

Many respectable people considered navvies to be so far outside civilised society that they established missions, centred on mission huts such as this one in Leicestershire. (*Leicestershire, Leicester and Rutland Record Office*)

Many workers in precarious employment, such as dockers, lived in adjacent lodging houses. In the early twentieth century those near Cardiff Docks were at the centre of a national scandal. (*Mark Fynn Postcards*)

Flower-selling was a common trade among women living in lodging houses, requiring little capital. (*Library of Congress*)

The country-wide growth of well-stocked shops such as this Co-operative Society shop in Walkden, Manchester, threatened the livelihood of the itinerant hawker. (*Mullineux Collection, Chetham's Library*)

Few types of convenience food could not be bought on the street. This man is selling sandwiches in Leicester. (*Leicestershire, Leicester and Rutland Record Office*)

There was an enormous market in second-hand clothes which were often sold by itinerant hawkers. (*Author's own collection*)

One of the numerous ways in which deserted children eked a living was as crossing-sweepers. This also gave them the opportunity to make a few coppers while running errands. (*Author's own collection*)

A similar situation was found in Wakefield in 1859 during a midnight tour of the local lodging houses. An entire bed could be had for 6*d* or a shared bed for 3*d*. This, as usual, conferred use of the kitchen but each lodger was required to provide his own soap and candle. Many of the lodgers were of a fearsome appearance: 'The coarse and in too many cases, brutal faces, distorted by sleep, looked weird and ghostly in the dim light of the candle.' Some of the sleepers were evidently in a drunken stupor. The air was generally 'close and offensive' and yet, except in a case where parents were sharing a bed with their children, there was little overcrowding. But for the lack of ventilation, conditions were generally 'tolerably good' and 'the bedrooms were cleanly whitewashed and the iron bedsteads could harbour nothing objectionable.'

The same investigator visited another house full of men who worked for the visiting fair and then went to 'a small house kept by an old woman as dirty as she was old'. The kitchen presented 'an indescribable scene of dirt and confusion' and in one of the bedrooms there was a mattress 'which would scarcely hang together' and a cupboard barely 2ft high, which was 'the sleeping place of a small boy'.

Others he visited were objectionable in various ways, and he found 'an utter disregard of the commonest decencies of life', such as single girls sleeping in the same rooms as married couples – something that was quite normal by working class standards of the day. Yet some were appalling by any standards: one old building seemed 'planted over a drain from which noxious effluvium penetrated the whole dwelling.' In another, 'all was dirt, stench and discomfort', reeking of overcrowded, unwashed bodies. He found many single women in these houses who invariably claimed to make a living as hawkers and many of the men claimed that they made a living hawking nuts.

He then went to the worst part of town, where 'house after house vied with each other as to which could best attract the lowest class of vagrant by dirt and dilapidated grimness.' Only in one house did he find separate rooms for those willing to pay for privacy. Otherwise there was 'the dreadful comingling of the sexes'. Most of the buildings he visited were no more than converted cottages.

As one seasoned traveller told Mayhew, sometimes these lodgings were so bad that 'you must get half-drunk or your money for your bed is wasted. There is so much rest owing to you after a hard day; and bugs and bad air'll prevent its being paid, if you don't lay in some stock or beer or liquor to sleep on. It's a duty you owes yourself.'

The Reverend George Edwards carried out a survey of cheap lodging accommodation in Preston in 1902. He found thirty-four houses, twenty-three of which took in women. They ranged from those with only a few beds to those that held over seventy people. They varied in quality but were generally better than in Wakefield forty years earlier. Other sources make it clear that there was a steady improvement throughout the second half of the century. One of the more unusual accounts was provided by George Davis of Hounslow.

Davis was clearly a man who would have felt at home in our litigious age. In 1880 he wrote to Scotland Yard complaining of the standard of accommodation available at the King's Head, a large beer house and lodging house in Staines. As a result an Inspector of Nuisances visited Davis, whose chief complaint was that he was cold at night. The inspector, however, found 'beds of oat chaff, a bolster, pillow, two sheets, a covering consisting of patchwork quilting and wadding, four or five times thick and a counterpane', all of which were in 'a fair condition'.

A popular route for itinerants of every sort was that from London to Birmingham. It is worth retracing the route that so many trod in the mid-nineteenth century, as it gives a feel for the range of accommodation available and the variety of people likely to be encountered along the way. Going from one lodging house to the next involved walking between ten and twenty miles a day, something that to many of us today appears a great feat of athleticism. Our Victorian ancestors, however, were prodigious walkers: Dickens routinely walked twenty miles for leisure and was by no means an exception.

The average charge for a reasonable house on that route was 4*d* and less for the more basic provision. When custom was poor, the traveller enjoyed the luxury of an entire bed to himself, whereas at busy times, when there were fairs or race meetings in the area, he might count himself lucky to get any share of a bed.

The most popular lodging house in Romford, as was common in many towns, doubled as a public house. The King's Arms, like most lodging houses, provided a kitchen for cooking and a proper division of the married and single. With forty beds, some of which were surrounded by curtains, it was deemed respectable. Similarly, the main lodging house in Chelmsford was also a beershop. There, however, the resemblance ends for the Three Queens was not only 'a rickety place' but also a place where 'you could get a pint of beer and a punch of the head, all for 2d', as recorded by Mayhew. With only fourteen beds it was frequently overcrowded and made no pretence of respectability.

The Castle at Braintree was also a beershop, but one with a cosmopolitan flavour. One of its patrons described it as a place that 'takes all sorts and sizes; all colours and all nations'. With only twenty-two beds it separated men and women but was nevertheless not in the same class as the Rose and Crown at Thaxton, which was distinctly up-market. At 6d a night it was one of the more expensive houses and offered singing and patter in the taproom. It had only ten beds and was decent and comfortable.

Saffron Walden may be one of the most affluent places in Britain today but in the mid-nineteenth century its lodging house, The Castle was 'as slovenly as could be'. Its clientele was mixed, consisting of both tradesmen and 'moochers', though the two avoided interaction, as was common in most lodging houses where 'each stuck to his own'. Less reputable still was Yorkshire Betty's in Barnwell, Cambridge, where men and women were mixed in its thirty beds. Much smaller was the Woolpack at Newmarket, which had only six beds, but was described as 'a lively place'.

At Bury St Edmunds the intriguingly named Old Jack Something's was not to the liking of the disreputable. With only twelve beds, its proprietor ensured that it was always clean, comfortable and honest. The traveller passing through Mildenhall, however, might well find it hard to get shelter, as the only house was a private home with a mere seven beds.

A totally different establishment was the Tom and Jerry at Ely. A spartan place, unique in having no kitchen, the landlord was 'easily frightened' with the result that 'it was a regular rough place where there was often quarrelling all night long and any caper was allowed between men and women.' This points up the importance of firm management in a lodging house, as otherwise the inmates tended towards disruptive behaviour. The Plume of Feathers at St Ives, though bigger, was no better than 'passable'. Like many of these market town houses it was small, with only eleven beds.

Perhaps one of the most disreputable and dangerous houses was the Bell and Dickey at St Neots, noted, in the words of one patron, for its 'queer doings'. Being out of the way, much of what went on there was unnoticed and it attracted 'a body of men that don't like to run gaping to the beak'. Often there were three to a bed, men, women and children all intermingled. Its infamy, however, was exceeded by that of the Cock in Bedford, which was likened to the most squalid lodging houses in Whitechapel.

At the other extreme of respectability was a small house in Irchester, where bed before 9pm was the rule, described as 'hard and honest, clean and rough'. Accommodation in Wellington was also in a private house but it was far from orderly and became the venue of rogues and villains when the fair was on. One of the best on the route was Mrs Bull's, a private house which was not only comfortable and decent but a 'nice, quiet Sunday house' with twelve beds. The beds were good too at the private house offering accommodation in Market Harborough but otherwise the place was only 'middling'.

The private house where travellers stayed at Lutterworth, located above a shop, was nothing less than 'very queer', as lacking in comfort as in decency, and consisting of only ten beds. The proprietor of the Rookery in Leicester had a distinctly rustic approach to tackling the problem of a bed shortage, as described by Mayhew: he 'shakes up the beds with a pitchfork and brings in straw if there's more than can possibly be crammed into beds.' The Teaboard at Hinckley was much better, though smaller with only eight beds, and very comfortable. Similarly, the private house that offered beds at Nuneaton was small but snug.

Unfortunately, the same could not be said of Bill Cooper's in Coventry, which one visitor described as 'a dilapidated place and there's no sleep [in its twenty beds] for there's an army of bugs – great black fellows'. In nearby Birmingham things were a great deal better at Mrs Leach's 'comfortable and decent' house with thirty beds, but, like most big cities, Birmingham had its share of bad places.

In the smaller towns, however, there was often no choice as many had only a single lodging house. Consequently these places attracted the entire gamut of travellers, as Mayhew revealed, 'the beggar, the robber and the pick-pocket; the street patterer and the street trader; the musician, the ballad singer and the street performer; the diseased, the blind, the lame and the half-idiot; the outcast girl and the hardened prostitute; young and old and all complexions and all countries'. Cast together with them is the 'wearied mechanic, travelling in search of employment, and even the broken-down gentleman or scholar, whose means do not exceed 4d'.

Even this comprehensive list does not mention all those groups for whom lodging houses were important. Many single parents found accommodation there, as did blind people. The 1851 census records eighteen blind keepers, while some lodgers were mentally ill and elderly, many of whom were in receipt of outdoor relief. There is evidence that some lodging houses catered specifically for the elderly, such as that of Jonathan South, in Berrington Street, Hereford which in 1861 accommodated five people in their eighties and a man of ninety-nine. Few, however, were able to compete with John Pratt, who lived in a lodging house in Oxford in 1861, while in his hundred-and-sixth year.

These old people were often broken by a lifetime of relentless toil and too infirm to maintain themselves by their own labour. On the other hand, there was a significant element of the lodging house population who made it their life's work to avoid work. How did they survive?

Chapter Six

'Aint Eaten for Five Days': Beggars and Tramps

His head was pressed against the wet pavement and his back arched up, his arms and legs splayed and his eyes turned up in his head, with only the whites visible. A crowd formed a circle about him, transfixed by the blood oozing from his nose and the froth flecking his mouth and chin. But it was the choking noise, the gurgling in his throat as his tongue lolled on his chin that held the crowd silent. Then his body fell limp. But the gurgling sound continued and the blood glistened on his face.

Two women stepped into the circle and lifted him to his feet. They parked him on a low wall and bent to his ear, whispering reassurance.

'No wonder he's collapsed,' said one of the women. 'Poor dear aint eaten for five days.' The second woman took a sixpence from her purse and pressed it into the man's palm. She turned to the crowd.

'Will you see him starve?' she reproached. 'Will no one show a scrap of Christian charity to this poor creature?' They wilted under her unblinking gaze and fumbled in their pockets.

That evening, back in their Drury Lane lodging house, in a court within a court, the epileptic and his female companions counted their money. It had been a profitable day.

Throwing a fit was just one of the myriad ruses used by professional beggars. It was always important to choose a time and location carefully. Outside a church, just as the congregation was leaving, was ideal. By the time he told his sad story – often supported by a written testimonial from a minister of religion – his concerned helpers were pressing on him the proceeds of an impromptu collection.

John Fisher Murray visited a lodging house in 1844 where he found the ersatz epileptic and many other professional beggars – or 'gegors' as they called themselves. Fisher had to concede that the fraudster's use of soap, to produce the frothing at the mouth, and food dye pushed up his nostrils to produce the haemorrhaging, certainly added to the authenticity of his act. The ersatz epileptic was one of the numerous professional moochers whose aversion to work was such that they would expend any amount of ingenuity and effort to avoid it.

No one condemned these scroungers more vehemently than Henry Mayhew, as described in his seminal work on the underclass, *London Labour and the London Poor:*

> We are surrounded by wandering hordes, distinguished from the civilized man by his repugnance to regular and continuous labour and by want of providence in laying up a store for the future, by his inability to perceive consequences ever so slightly removed from immediate apprehension, by his passion for intoxicating liquors, by his extraordinary powers of enduring privations, by his comparative insensibility to pain, by an immoderate love of gambling, by his love of libidinous dances, by the absence of chastity among his women and his disregard of female honour, by his vague sense of religion.

Every commentator agreed that drunkenness 'appears to have been first and foremost a cause and a condition of the tramp's existence'. There is no doubt that a a sober tramp was as rare as a warm and welcoming casual ward. In the 1890s five times as many people died of alcohol-related illnesses than did sixty years later. Those with experience of the tramp life at the end of the nineteenth century estimate that between ninety and ninety-five per cent of tramps were alcoholics. This is supported by the fact that habitués of the casual wards were at this time almost twice as likely as the general population to die of alcohol abuse.

Nor it is possible to claim that tramps were poor unfortunates cursed with low intelligence or mental illness. A Manchester study concluded that dossers were no less intelligent than the average working man, but that in ninety per cent of cases 'yielding to drink has been the start of their degradation'. The Royal Commission on the Care and Control of the Feeble-Minded at the beginning of the twentieth century found that only five per cent of the inmates of the casual wards fell into this category.

Even the most compassionate philanthropists stressed the viciousness and dishonesty of beggars and asserted that the deserving poor never resorted to begging, which was the exclusive vocation of idle rogues and vagabonds who abused Christian charity. If professional beggars were permitted to benefit from charity, they argued, the moral order was turned on its head. Only those who are poor through no fault of their own deserve charity and even that must not be unconditional. It must be paid for with labour. If not, what incentive is there for the poor to work? If not, idleness and deceit are rewarded and ultimately the whole moral order collapses.

One reason for this unsentimental attitude was the ubiquity of beggars. The professional beggar was as common in Victorian cities and towns as the horse. He formed a distinct sub-class of the great nomadic tribe constantly on the move. He was at the bottom of the criminal hierarchy and regarded begging as a craft, a trade at which he worked in order to improve his income.

Despite appearances to the contrary, beggars were far from the pathetic, isolated individuals they presented to the public; in fact they were part of a fellowship which shared best practice. It is no coincidence that accounts of beggars' strategies in different parts of the country are remarkably similar; the same ploys appeared in Manchester and Newcastle as in London and Bristol.

Though commentators were unanimous in condemning these charlatans, the public attitude was far more ambivalent. Britain's long Christian tradition meant people esteemed charity and the charitable. Many were sympathetic to their plight and the poor were particularly generous to them – especially when under the influence of alcohol. Yet there was also a widespread fear of tramps as carriers of disease and many felt intimidated into giving them something, if only to get rid of them. Besides, tramps were widely believed to wreak vengeance on those who turned them away empty-handed, especially in rural areas where they reputedly burnt outhouses and crops in revenge against those who refused them charity.

Many sexual assaults were laid at their door too and they were widely regarded as incorrigible thieves who would steal anything that came to hand. Nonetheless, they were also the beneficiaries of a certain amount of maudlin sentimentality, expressed in poems and songs that suggested that the tramp's life was without cares or mundane concerns.

The problem of a wandering population of homeless people was exacerbated by the introduction of the new Poor Law system in Ireland in 1838, at a time when it was estimated that between two and three million people there were dependent on begging or were destitute for part of the year. As thousands of Irish seasonal workers arrived in Britain – most travelling as ballast in the holds of returning coal vessels – they brought with them droves of beggars; many of the workers begged while travelling to somewhere they hoped to get work. It was usual for the men to travel first, followed by their wives and children, who also begged their way to where their husbands were working.

The Vagrancy Act of 1824 made begging illegal and gave the authorities the power to prosecute under one of three categories – idle and disorderly, rogues and vagabonds or incorrigible rogues – with each liable to a sentence of up to a year's imprisonment. Each of these terms had a legal definition. The 'idle and disorderly' were those who failed to provide for their family, refused to work or begged in their parish of settlement. 'Rogues and vagabonds' were professional beggars who operated outside their parish of settlement, men who had abandoned their families and forced them to rely on poor relief, some travelling entertainers and fortune tellers, 'reputed' thieves' and 'suspect persons', that is, those who loitered around the streets and were apparently up to no good. The 'incorrigible rogue' was the recidivist, the person who had previously been convicted as a rogue or vagabond and shown no inclination to mend his ways.

The Act also gave the authorities the power to search lodging houses and immediately there was a jump in the number of vagrants jailed. But prosecutions could do nothing in the face of the human catastrophe unfolding in the wake of the Irish Famine. In 1847 alone 250,000 Irish paupers arrived in Liverpool. Even after the Famine influx ended, seasonal begging and vagrant immigrants remained a fixture during the second half of the nineteenth century.

Vagrants are not to be confused with casual labourers, with whom they often shared beds in lodging houses. Many vagrants did occasionally resort to honest labour when there was no alternative, yet the perambulations of the vagrant were entirely different from those of the genuine job seeker. Tramps did not wander aimlessly but often followed well-worn routes. They left the cities in April, as the weather improved, and launched out into the countryside. As soon as the days began to shorten, they wended their way to the big cities where indiscriminate charity and free accommodation were most readily had. Once there, many wintered in common lodging houses or shelters for the homeless and passed the day begging, holding horses or carrying parcels from piers and railway stations. Some got the occasional day's work on a market or made a few shilling by scavenging for goods they could sell to marine stores.

Some gravitated to seaside resorts during the summer, where holidaymakers, giddy with the joys of recreation, were likely to be generous to a man 'down on his luck'. Others made for the hop fields of Kent and Sussex where extra labour was always in demand during the picking season. As one professional moocher confessed with disarming frankness, 'the work is not hard and there are a great many loose girls to be found there'.

Brighton, with its constant supply of affluent visitors, became a magnet for beggars, and in response to their peculiar needs a host of lodging houses sprang up. Their keepers sold trifles wholesale to the faux peddlers, financed robberies and supplied the newly arrived professional beggars with information on soft-touches and profitable begging grounds.

Various surveys of the tramp population, estimated at between 20,000 and 30,000 in 1900, suggest that only about one–sixth used casual wards. A century earlier an eminent magistrate, Patrick Colquhoun, estimated that there were 90,000 of these peripatetics; 70,000 tramps, beggars and gypsies, 10,000 wandering performers and 'dubious peddlers' and the same number employed in selling lottery tickets. During the first two decades of the nineteenth century crime escalated to a terrifying extent, resulting in the establishment of a modern police force with the creation of the Metropolitan Police in 1829. Added to this there were in good times 10,000 and in bad 50,000 workers moving in search of employment. Police statistics for the period 1857 to 1868 show that the number of tramps known to them varied from 33,000 to 36,000. In 1868 there were 5,648 known 'tramps' lodging-houses'. The 1906 Departmental Committee on Vagrancy estimated that ten per cent of the occupants of London's lodging houses were tramps.

Nothing attracted wandering beggars like indiscriminate charity, which drew professional scroungers from far and wide. Particularly attractive to the moocher was free accommodation. In Oxford, for instance, a hostel for the homeless was opened in Castle Street in 1847. Before long it took on the character of a 'hotel for tramps', attracted undesirables of all hues and aroused the ire of local residents. Even those casual wards which operated a lax regime attracted scroungers. When new casual wards were added to Oxford's Cowley Road workhouse in 1882 they must have operated in a laid-back and undemanding manner, as they soon attracted between 4,000 and 5,000 tramps a year. Conversely, the professional scrounger very quickly learnt to avoid those tramp wards which operated a rigorous regime.

Neither the night shelters, which sprang up in most big cities, nor food distribution centres were without their critics as many complained that they made no effort to determine the needs of those they helped: the unemployed worker and professional scrounger were treated identically. Neither was required to do anything in return for charity, with the inevitable result that these places became magnets for the feckless idlers who preyed on the benevolence of the naive. In fact, the Liverpool refuge was closed in 1848 as it was swamped by scroungers and particularly prostitutes. The police reports of every major city and town of the period contain complaints about the baleful effects of the tendency of charitable institutions to attract criminals and outcasts.

Towards the end of the nineteenth century public emergency appeals, similar to the Lord Mayor's Mansion House appeal, first launched in 1819, and backed by local and national newspapers, became a commonplace response to virtually every downturn in trade. The problem was that the distribution of the proceeds was invariably haphazard, offering ample scope for the practised scrounger. The 1864 Select Committee on Poor Relief recorded numerous instances of beggars abusing the system by, for instance, exchanging bread they had been given for drink. Pub landlords then sold it at reduced prices to their customers. It is estimated that at least a quarter of the £2 million raised to relieve the Lancashire Cotton Famine of 1861 to 1863 was defrauded.

Similarly, the Lords' Select Committee of 1888 cited manifold instances of charitable aid serving only to line the pockets of landlords and to attract avaricious fraudsters and professional scroungers from far afield. When philanthropists started handing out coffee and bread to those sleeping rough around Trafalgar Square in 1889, the number of down and outs in the area immediately swelled from 20 to 400, instantly swamping all the casual wards in the area. The Charity Organisation carried out a study of these same casual wards and night shelters over the next two years and concluded that only a minute fraction of the cases were deserving.

Charity is to beggars what the sea is to a swimmer: without one the other is impossible. Despite the impression created by many commentators, charity was central to the lives of people of all stations in Victorian society. It was, after all, widely acknowledged as a Christian's duty to his fellow man. In 1882 one Poor Law guardian calculated that working people gave beggars at least twenty times more then they donated to official charities. One estimate reckons that professional scroungers benefitted to the tune of about £8.5 million in 1869. London's charitable donations during the 1880s exceeded total government expenditure on the Royal Navy.

The way in which charities operated made it easy for the undeserving to exploit the generosity of compassionate hearts: there was little or no coordination between the plethora of philanthropic outlets. Churches and sects, organisations and individuals vied to outdo each other in largesse. The professional scrounger could go from one food charity to another, eating his fill and selling the rest in a lodging house. Similarly, at a time when there was a buoyant market in second-hand clothes, it paid the enterprising tramp to retain tattered garments as his 'working clothes', as his rags invariably elicited an offer of a coat or a pair of trousers which he promptly sold.

What made it difficult for the discerning benefactor to identify the deserving cause was the limitless ingenuity of beggars who were practised in every nuance of heart-string pulling. They were seldom mute implorers, merely extending an importuning hand. They invariably had a patter, a hard luck story to encourage generosity. Their approach was sharpened, many believed, by their acquaintance with the better class of eloquent rogue they encountered in lodging houses.

When it came to begging, women had a great advantage over their male counterparts. Though most beggars were men, many women ploughed the same furrow. The majority were failed prostitutes or servants who had been sacked and could not, without a 'character', get another job. George Atkins Brine, known as the King of the Beggars, candidly admitted that the sexual licence tramps enjoyed was one of the lifestyle's chief attractions. Female tramps usually hooked up with a male counterpart, moving from town to town, often staying at those lodging houses totally dependent on the patronage of beggars, before eventually going their separate ways.

Man or woman, adult or child, every beggar had his own modus operandi. The ingenuity of those who lived by duping others could equal the creativity of the greatest minds of the time. Few members of the public could resist the appeal of whimpering children, blue with cold and pinched with hunger or the tale of the returned missionary, one of the more elaborate scams. The beauty of this was that it exploited the public's insatiable fascination with darkest Africa, missionaries and exploration of Britain's Empire. Sometimes known as the professional prater or bogus preacher, he needed a group of helpers to create the sort of heady atmosphere in which generosity overwhelmed prudence. Four or five enthusiastic members of the audience, properly primed, would generate interest and, together with a few banners and a couple of musicians, a large crowd soon gathered. Then it was up to the prater to work his magic.

For the best effect he had a converted African demonstrate his enthusiasm for Christianity by spitting on a pagan idol, before leading the assembled throng in a stirring rendition of 'Onward Christian Soldiers'. Almost as an afterthought, a collection was taken up and the crowd dispersed, happy in the knowledge that they were helping to spread the light of the Gospel.

A significant section of the begging community consisted of the writers of begging letters. These practitioners came from the higher echelons of the begging fraternity; they were literate and capable of the research necessary to ensure that they targeted those likely to be most responsive. Many badgered public figures while the more perceptive chose local philanthropists and those prominent in charitable organisations. Renowned philanthropists, clergymen of all hues, public figures, winners of lotteries and other publicised prize-winners were all favoured targets. Charles Dickens was only one of the public figures they plagued. Each presented a carefully developed persona: one was a distressed gentlewoman, another an officer's widow; the ship-wrecked mariner, the disabled miner, unable to work after an explosion at the coal-face, and the impoverished gardener struggling in winter were all standard characters.

One group of begging letter-writers whose activities came to light in 1850 worked out of Wards' lodging house in Rag Row, Banbury, and consisted of a woman, a one-legged man and a one-armed man. This sort of crime was common among clerks who had come down in the world –

usually as a result of their dishonesty – who were a staple of many lodging houses.

The more audacious followed up their letter with a visit, during which a refusal to give money resulted in tears, hysterics and tantrums calculated to create such embarrassment that the victim was willing to pay the overwrought scrounger to get rid of them. More despicable still were those who targeted the recently bereaved. By trawling the obituary notices they found suitable targets, often respectable women who had recently lost their husbands. The letter-writer purported to be a former lover supported by the deceased. Implicit in the letter was the threat to make the matter public and in the majority of cases the family was glad to pay up in order to prevent any illicit relationship becoming public.

Far subtler was the beggar who used neither the written nor the spoken word, but dressed in clothes that spoke of threadbare respectability. He usually entered a pub in a respectable working class area and looking suitably doleful, made an inept attempt to sell something of little worth – a box of matches or some tobacco – which he maintained was his only hope of raising a few coppers. As soon as someone engaged him in conversation he would recount his heart-rending tale of cruel misfortune. The astute practitioner of this ruse found it worked best on a Saturday evening when the pub was full of women having a drink after completing their shopping. Generally they still had a few shillings in their purses and were feeling, for the only occasion in the week, quite decently off. This well-being was likely to overflow into generosity.

Disabled beggars did well but the most successful were the disfigured – the more shocking the wound, the better the impact. The ability to simulate wounds was an art as valuable as any trade or practical skill. A thick layer of soap plastered onto the arm or thigh needed only an application of vinegar to ensure that it blistered and appeared for all the world like a running wound. Similarly, a piece of raw meat tied under a clotted dressing invariably melted the hardest heart. Healed amputations guaranteed a beggar a regular income. Soap, strong vinegar and blood squeezed from raw meat and applied to the stump created such a realistic weeping sore that most passers-by averted their eyes while dropping coins into the beggar's cup. A brisk massage with gunpowder gave the skin the colour of decaying, inflamed flesh and was a great bonus to anyone whose living depended on arousing sympathy.

In fact, Victorian beggars showed keen insights. They knew that respectable people attached great importance to wearing sufficient clothing: apart from considerations of decency, it was believed that insufficient clothing was a major cause of ill health. One group of beggars sought to exploit this by calling door to door, while half-naked, asking for food and clothing. They realised people were more likely to give them old clothes – easily converted into cash – than money. Most of these beggars worked one prosperous suburban area after another. Occasionally, they varied their approach, posing as a travelling workman who had the promise of a job but would not be taken on in rags.

But the most productive door-to-door beggars were women, preferably accompanied by respectably dressed children, ideally little lisping girls. Beggars in Manchester's Strangeways area used little girls for many years. The child would accost an adult and ask for money. Almost immediately the adult partner would appear and reproach the victim for using foul language to the child. Soon the allegation was stepped up and the adult demanded money if he was not to report the matter to the police.

The static beggar, standing on a corner, his hand pitifully beseeching a copper, was unlikely to succeed. The competition was too tough. That type of begging was monopolised by apparently respectable women, children and cripples. The police were likely to arrest or move on a man adopting this unimaginative approach, so a prop was necessary to avoid this fate. Consequently, many carried a hawker's tray, selling needles or matches, which were merely a pretext for aggressive begging. A placard, setting out the heart-breaking circumstances under which the wearer was crippled, was another favoured prop.

A white stick was also effective. Blindness was quite common among the poor, the result of industrial accidents, smallpox and untreated gonorrhoea. The obedient dog, lying by his master, was a common sight all over Britain. But a far better prop was a child acting as a guide. Feigning a medical condition allowed beggars to use their acting talents. Most of those with dramatic tendencies went in for fit throwing. Some alcoholics feigned collapse near a pub in the hope that some compassionate soul would fetch 6*d* worth of brandy to revive them.

The shrewd beggar was well informed, and used events in the news to give his sorry tale a veneer of credibility. So, a man crippled in a recent pit disaster or bereft of his family and all his possessions after a shipwreck which was the talk of the town was sure to evoke sympathy.

Joseph Dare was fascinated by the variety of rogues he encountered in Leicester's lodging houses in the 1850s. In particular, he was intrigued by what he called the 'high-flyers', educated men who would claim acquaintance with genteel families as part of a ruse to ingratiate themselves to respectable men whom they proceeded to fleece. At the other end of the scale were the 'forney-squarers' who made fake gold rings which they sold to servant girls or sometimes exchanged for food and clothing.

The 'Widow's Lark', involved a woman posing as a bereaved mother – sometimes borrowing children to create the desired impression. She played on the sympathies of all she encountered, frequently using the proceeds to support a feckless husband. Others who relied on their ability to tell a heart-rending tale were the 'gridlers' and 'chanters', whose misfortunes would even engage the sympathies of a pawnbroker. The gridlers specialised in singing psalms and thus adding credibility to their accounts of blameless lives blighted by cruel misfortune. Describing one pair of gridlers, an observer commented that 'in your entire life you never saw a brace of such sanctimonious rascals'. They worked only Dissenting neighbourhoods, hoping there to more readily arouse the sympathy of the godly.

So ubiquitous were rogues who played on others' generosity that many respectable Victorians were afflicted by charity fatigue. Pestering by professional beggars was more than a minor annoyance – it was regarded by the successive chief constables of Manchester, for instance, as a major problem, so great in fact that no less a person than Jerome Caminada was deputed to put an end to it. The legendary detective, regarded by many as the real-life inspiration for the character of Sherlock Holmes, set about resolving the problem with his customary gusto.

Most Manchester beggars at that time were women who would walk beside a person wailing a pitiable tale. So persistent were they that their actions amounted to a form of blackmail.

One night shortly before 11pm, as Caminada was walking along Oxford Street, near Manchester city centre, he came across a known beggar, Soldier Mary Ann, who appeared to be comforting a child swathed in her shawl. Unaware of Caminada, she latched on to a couple emerging from the Prince's Theatre and immediately launched into her patter, recounting her piteous tale of a deserted wife who had walked from Liverpool in a fruitless attempt to locate her wayward husband and now had no means of feeding or sheltering her hungry child.

At this point Caminada intervened. The baby turned out to be a young boy – who immediately took to his heels. His parents hired him out as a heart-rending prop for 3*d* a night. Mary Ann had so many previous convictions that she was sentenced to twelve months with hard labour. Her case deserves more detailed consideration, as she is typical of many of Manchester's professional beggars of the period.

Mary Ann was a woman of many aliases. This, of course, was common among criminals of all sorts, who hoped to avoid the heavier penalties imposed on habitual offenders by adopting multiple identities. Mary Ann's real name was Ann Ryan and her offences included theft; when threatened with arrest she was quite happy to resort to violent resistance. On one occasion, when arrested for stealing corsets, she tried to fight off the police. Between 1873 and 1889 she was convicted of begging, drunkenness, breach of the peace and being drunk and disorderly. She was in every respect the typical street beggar of the time.

Another famous Manchester policeman, James Bent, renowned for charitable work with the city's poor over many years, tells of a professional beggar operating in Davyhulme, where he was pretending to be a mute miner. The magistrate sentenced him to three months' imprisonment.

Another professional beggar posed as an invalid – he wore shoes on his hands and dragged himself along on all fours. He received six weeks.

Many beggars combined importuning with hawking or street entertainment. Very often there was only the finest of lines between these activities. Selling matches or pins was often a pretext for accosting someone in the street and compelling him to listen to a well-rehearsed hard luck story. It also provided a reason for hanging about while looking for the opportunity to steal from a passing cart or a shop's footpath display. A great deal of this sort of petty crime was the work of beggars. In fact, the Manchester police estimated that two-thirds of all crime was down to vagrants.

Long before Caminada was set to rid Manchester's streets of beggars, the activities of professional scroungers caused such widespread disquiet that in 1818 concerned citizens founded the Society for the Suppression of Mendacity, to ensure that charity reached the deserving poor. Though later characterised as hard-hearted and callous, many of its members were active in charitable works and the Society itself provided much help for the needy. Its view was that those who gave to beggars had no way of distinguishing the genuine from the bogus poor and, as most beggars were professional scroungers, money given did nothing to help the deserving but instead encouraged idleness and dishonesty.

The idea caught on and eventually similar societies emerged all over the country. Each member was equipped with a book of relief tickets which he distributed in place of alms. The recipients presented these at one of the societies' many offices, where they were interviewed. If deemed deserving they received food, overnight accommodation and perhaps money. Additionally, many of these societies employed officers to patrol the streets, distributing tickets to the genuine and handing over frauds to the police. In 1869 the Mendicity Society introduced a Bread Tickets Scheme to discourage alms-giving, whereby subscribers gave the tickets to beggars who then redeemed them against food at one of its many centres throughout the country.

The first such society claimed that by 1834 it had reduced the number of beggars in Bath by ninety per cent. The London Society for the Suppression of Mendicity had an annual income of £4,000 by 1860 and employed eight patrol officers. In the course of its work it built up a register of beggars, accumulating details of 72,000 by 1900, which it used to prosecute frauds. On the other hand it also distributed free meals, as many as 239,000 in some years during the 'hungry forties'.

But even the distribution of free food was problematic. In 1871 the Charity Organisation Society condemned soup kitchens, asserting that they encouraged beggars and bemoaned the growth in night shelters which served only to confirm the addiction of the idle and feckless to a life on charity. 'If you wish to relieve genuine poverty,' it told the public, 'you will find the means through the clergyman, the Little Sisters of the Poor or the relieving officer. In the streets you will find nothing but the professional toll takers, levying dues on personal weakness.' The Society encouraged the public to issue street beggars with tickets which they were to present at its offices, where the deserving would get aid in the form of money, blankets and clothing. They also claimed to offer suitable employment to every able-bodied beggar.

The London Mendicity Society also undertook to follow up begging letters, which were a major source of income for the literate beggar. By 1900 it had a collection of 229,000 such missives. The competent 'screever' was reputed to earn £5 a week in the 1870s, the equivalent of a professional salary. As late as 1905 George Sims reported that some lodging houses were home to syndicates of screevers, who operated on a cooperative basis and Rowton Houses in particular were much favoured by such groups as management would not allow the police access.

As for beggars who worked the streets, there was considerable debate about how much they made. Mayhew estimated that a mid-nineteenth-century beggar earned about 8s a week, roughly equal to the wage of a farm labourer. In 1869 the Secretary of the Howard Association, the predecessor of the Howard League for Penal Reform, estimated that the figure was at least one pound and that many begging families earned more than curates, clerks or schoolteachers.

Visiting a lodging house situated 'in a court within a court' near Drury Lane in 1844, John Fisher Murray was mesmerised by the ingenuity of the tricksters he encountered. The house, which had originally consisted of five small houses, kept its best beds for superior visitors, namely 'begging letter writers, the lower class of imposters and swindlers, sneaks and pickpockets'.

Some screevers did not send their pleas through the post but accosted passers-by with letters of recommendation, usually from a notable public figure or clergyman. These testified to the bearer's good character and commended him to the public as a deserving recipient of charity. Such testimonials were much in demand and their production provided discredited lawyers and alcoholic clerks with a meagre income.

In addition to throwing light on the activity of screevers, the Mendicity Society's records also make clear the large number of children involved in begging. Child beggars outnumbered adults, though police and other official records underestimate the extent of their involvement because they enjoyed a degree of impunity not shared by adults. The police were loath to arrest them as magistrates were often at a loss how to treat them and usually sent them away with a warning, knowing full well that they would immediately resume begging. If a child's parents were imprisoned for sending them begging, then they were sent to the workhouse. But masters were reluctant to take young children and if the magistrates sent every beggar there they would have swamped the whole Poor Law system.

What then happened to these children, rejected by even the workhouse?

Chapter Seven

'Put a Man's Eye Out with a Poker': Children

If a man who died in the mid-nineteenth century were restored to life and dropped down in the middle of any of our thronging cities, he would be instantly overwhelmed by the differences between his day and ours. If we asked him to focus solely on people he would be amazed by their height – on average 5in taller than in his day – and their monstrous girths: people in the nineteenth century were far more likely to be under weight than obese. But what would strike him most forcefully is the absence of children. Where are all the children? In 1841 they made up forty per cent of the population; today they are a mere twenty per cent.

Children thronged the streets of every nineteenth century city and town. They ran along the pavements, whooping and jumping, flaying spinning tops and rolling hoops. The very idea of working class children sitting at home was anathema to parents. Their place was on the streets. But many were not playing: they were engaged in business. Their shrill voices screeched the latest headlines, telling of wars and disasters, salacious court cases and brutal slayings. They sold peas, ham sandwiches, soup, oysters and all the other myriad convenience foods of the day. They peddled matches and needles, herbs and flowers, swept crossings, ran errands and held horses. They delivered groceries and carried bags, cleaned chimneys and polished shoes.

What is less well known, however, is that many lived independently in lodging houses, without any parental supervision. They formed a significant element of those who would otherwise have been consigned to the workhouse. In many cases they remained in the area where they were born. In Oxford's St Thomas' lodging houses forty per cent of lodgers were born in the city or the surrounding countryside, and this seems to have been fairly typical of houses serving rural areas.

The bequest of the Industrial Revolution was a great deal more than factories and transport. It dealt a blow to traditional social structures, not least the family. One of the consequences of a burgeoning population during the agricultural revolution, which reduced the amount of labour needed on the land, was the advent of juvenile crime and begging on a level that aroused great concern among the political and social elite. Orphaned and abandoned children took to the streets where they wheedled a living, their only resource their wits. Estimates put the number at 16,000 immediately after the Napoleonic Wars and by 1848 there were believed to be no less than 30,000 in London alone, while all cities and towns had their share of street children.

Younger children were much sought after by professional beggars as there were few so hard-hearted that they could resist the wide-eyed gaze of a famished child, especially if blind or crippled. Some of these unfortunates were foreign children, the victims of their unscrupulous countrymen who were traffickers. The Italian scoundrels who specialised in this exploitation were known as *padroni* and their modus operandi was always the same: they approached parents, most often in the impoverished south of Italy, promising, for a fee, to take their child to England and train him to earn a living. Once in England the children were reduced to a state of slavery, forced to beg or work as organ grinders or street entertainers.

One notorious rascal, Giuseppe Delicato, filled lodging houses in Birmingham, Plymouth and Hanley with children he acquired by this means and who were reputedly able to earn as much as 10*s* a day by the 1890s. When some of his charges ran away, Delicato, with breath-taking audacity, advertised, offering a reward for their return. The problem was so serious that the Italian government legislated against the trade and the Italian Benevolent Society worked in Britain to find and return its victims. It was assumed that the problem of child exploitation would diminish with the 1876 Education Act, which compelled parents to send their children to school until they were ten, but many observers felt that the only change was that fewer children were exploited by *padronis* and more by their parents. A small number of German criminals also operated the same scam in their country, consigning their victims to lodging houses in the small German colony in Whitechapel.

Nevertheless, most of what James Greenwood described as an 'immense army of juvenile vagrants' were indigenous and he and Howard Goldsmid were appalled by the conditions many of them endured in lodging houses. Hundreds roamed the streets of Manchester and the authorities were seriously concerned by the scale of the problem. As late as 1889 a Manchester survey found 700 street children in the city, while in 1871 children under the age of 15 made up more than a quarter of the inmates of lodging houses in St Thomas' parish, Oxford. Barnardo's estimate confirms this: he believed that almost one in four dossers in registered lodging houses was under 16.

Writing of Leicester, Joseph Dare found that one of the problems of the city's lodging houses was that many of the lodgers were children who had been forced out of their homes because of overcrowding. Generally these were the unfortunates pushed away from the fireside and forced to resort to the warmth of the public house. Even among the best of working men it was quite common for their children to sleep at a neighbour's house if they had no room in their own.

Though young, these children of the lodging houses did not defer to their elders in infamy. W.H. Davies, the renowned 'super-tramp', was convinced that the most dangerous occupants of lodging houses were these 'half-boys, half-men'. Any house that harboured them was a hazardous place to live as it was these youths who, more than any group, made 'the slums of London and other large cities so dangerous'. They were 'distinguished from full-grown men by their total recklessness. They will lift a poker at the slightest provocation and are as quick to use a lethal weapon as to use their fists.' He recounts an incident when such a youth put out the eye of an old man on the flimsiest of pretexts.

Nineteenth century research into the background of these children reveals unsurprising results. Many were the children of criminals and had been abandoned by both parents. A combination of the deserted, the orphaned and the runaway, the vast majority were illegitimate offspring driven out to beg and steal. Some had absconded from refuges for homeless children, such as Barnes' House in Salford. Once on the streets they relied on the common lodging house, whose keeper was often a receiver of the goods they stole.

They were forced onto the streets or into lodging houses because, as the chaplain of Manchester Gaol testified in 1853, it was extremely difficult for lone children to get poor relief. When the Marquis of Granby lodging house, attached to the public house of the same name in Warwick town, was inspected in 1869, it had seventeen lodgers, including five children in bed or on the floor in each of its three rooms and 'all appeared to be tramps'. John Martin, a mid-nineteenth century criminal put his dishonest life down to the company he met in such a house in one of Manchester's most notorious areas, Blakely Street. These boys induced him to run away from his mother and become a professional thief. Another habitual criminal similarly blamed his demise on those he met in a lodging house in Banister Street, Birkenhead.

In using both in-depth and group interviews to discover the backgrounds of these lodging house children, Henry Mayhew was far in advance of his time. In January 1850 he brought together 150 of the 'lowest class of male juvenile thieves and vagabonds who infest the metropolis and the country at large'. All were under the age of 20 – one was just 6 and and many displayed the shaven head of the recently released convict. Of the total, eighty were orphans and only nineteen had both parents living. There were fifty beggars and sixty-six thieves. Only twenty-two were runaways and more than half of them wandered around the country every year, yet only a third slept regularly in casual wards and slightly fewer used tramps' lodging houses.

Of those who could read – sixty-three – nearly all had read tales of celebrated criminals and the illiterate had had the stories read to them, usually around the lodging house fire; all expressed delight in such exploits. This fascination with Dick Turpin, Jack Sheppard and other legendary desperados who were young criminals' heroes was widespread and found in lodging houses all over the country. The young swapped tales of the characters' audacity in kitchens and prison cells and sang about them in the pubs, beerhouses and the penny gaffs frequented by criminals. From the mid-century hawkers sold cheap written accounts of their exploits.

Mayhew found that many of the group he interviewed had their own adventures and tragedies to recount, like the Birmingham child who fled to London after enduring years of beatings. He fed himself by hawking trifles around the streets. 'This attraction of a street career is very strong,' Mayhew said, 'among the neglected children of the poor.' For these children the lodging house was an extension of the streets, a place where they were subject to no adult control and could do as they like provided they could afford to pay. After a short time living in this environment they often became proficient thieves and were irredeemably corrupted.

Many of Mayhew's respondents confirmed the importance of the lodging house as a breeding ground for young thieves. 'Without such places,' one told him, 'my trade could not be carried on', and that 'if any innocent boy gets into a lodging house he'll not be innocent long.'

Like most criminals, they were constantly on the move and they loved the anonymity of the big cities. Some were the children of lodgers while resident beggars and thief masters kept others they were training up for criminal gain. But many were alone. Their attitude to making a living was just what we would expect of a child. They were concerned with making enough for today, for their immediate needs, with little thought for tomorrow.

There were plenty of older criminals who regarded themselves as craftsmen, passing on their lore to the next generation, enabling them to make a living. Often, however, this was more self-interest than philanthropy. In many cases the mentor ran a lodging house and provided his charges with pencils, oranges, notebooks or other items they might peddle as a front for stealing.

It was often easier for such children to make a living than their adult counterparts. There was an insatiable demand for boy labour throughout the entire Victorian era. Youths cost less than adults, were more amenable and could simply be discarded when they reached maturity. They worked as errand boys, shops boys, van boys, delivery boys and performed countless mechanical tasks that made up the manufacture of most commodities.

Information presented to the House of Commons in 1899 detailed the employment of boys leaving London schools that year and found that forty per cent of them became errand boys, eight per cent office boys and junior clerks and eighteen per cent went into the building, metal, clothing and woodworking trades. Most of these jobs were of the classic dead-end type, offering no development and no improvement in wages. The future was inevitable: at some stage they would be turned out to join the great pool of causal labour and a lifetime of underemployment.

It was accepted by everyone familiar with this issue that virtually all the youths living in these places were not in regular employment but made their living on the streets, generally peddling one commodity or another. It's difficult for us today to visualise the clamour and noise of the streets, the great seething mass of incessantly moving humanity, ebbing and flowing along pavements and roads. There were few things you could not buy on the streets. Hawkers offered nuts, oranges, fresh flowers, dried flowers, herbs and lavender. For as little as a 1s it was possible for a hawker to buy a day's stock.

When the summer ended and there was no demand for certain seasonal goods, the hawker turned to other items: combs, stay laces, cedar pencils and watercress. Some were sold from arm baskets or a 'shallow' hanging from string around the neck or a small tin tray.

Much food was sold on the streets. Among the camestibles sold were fish – both wet and fresh, dry, smoked, cured, and shellfish – fruit and vegetables and 'green stuff' – watercress, chickweed and groundsel. There was always a demand for food that could be eaten on the run: ham sandwich-sellers worked the streets around theatres and music halls, while muffin-sellers covered their wares with a flannel cloth as punters preferred them warm. Crumpets were popular from September to spring. Fried fish, hot eels, pickled whelks, sheep's trotters, pea soup, hot green peas, penny pies, plum duff, meat puddings, baked potatoes, spice cakes, Chelsea buns, sweetmeats, brandy balls, cough drops and even meat for cats and dogs were all available from street vendors.

Oysters were among the most popular and cheapest fast foods of the day. The enterprising street seller set up his improvised stall, which might be no more than an upturned box, wherever he liked and sold them four for a penny, already opened and garnished with vinegar and pepper. On average, these people made between 4s and 10s a week, barely enough to ward off starvation and maintain a tenuous hold on existence.

For those in need of a drink to wash down their food, there was tea and coffee, ginger beer, lemonade, hot wine, new milk and curds and whey for sale on the street. Pastries provided a whole sub-class of street food: there were fruit pies, boiled meat and kidney puddings, plum puddings and a vast variety of tarts, cakes, buns and biscuits. From the 1870s there were also numerous sellers of that exotic continental delicacy, ice cream, usually Italian. At the bottom of the thoroughfare traders were the match-sellers.

A number of children also survived by scavenging. 'Waste not, want not' was the motto of those who were most in want. These children trawled the river banks in search of coal, metal, rope and bones which could be turned into a few coppers at a marine store.

Mayhew claimed that most children who were street hawkers were also thieves or beggars. Many did not have the wit to survive on the proceeds of theft. Invariably, these 'soft' creatures, often 'half fools', fell into begging, whereas their more astute fellows simply used begging as a pretext for stealing. Many of these children and young men had stolen first from their employers and then found that without a 'character' no one would employ them or worse still, their parents had driven them from home. It was at this stage that they came upon the lodging house and were inducted into a life of crime, which suggests that they were usually thieves before they had any experience of the lodging house.

One such urchin recounted how, in the 1850s, he met up with a group of men who passed themselves off as wounded soldiers, veterans of the Spanish Legion – the equivalent of the French Foreign Legion – and travelled the country begging and living in lodging houses. After a brief spell of imprisonment he tried to employ the techniques he had learnt from his mentors and posed as a 'turnpike sailor' and other victims of misfortune, making a good living and seldom having to work. He was adamant that there was once a time when an accomplished beggar could make as much as three guineas a week, but that time had passed and it was all even an old hand could do to feed himself.

Yet he also maintained that many lodging houses were totally dependent on the patronage of beggars. In such places beggars shared the mysteries of their trade, including information about villages and individual houses which had proved profitable. The 'cadgers' then had their own secret language or cant, which was entirely different from that of thieves and operated on the rhyming principle – examples of which are 'Jack surpass' for glass, 'finger and thumb' for rum and 'heaps of coke' for smoke.

During the 1890s the national press was full of accounts of the activities of 'street Arabs' or hooligans marauding round Manchester and terrorising the population. Local newspapers spoke of the Scuttlers – youth gangs based on loyalty to a specific area of the city – reducing the streets of the slums to a state of anarchy, where law-abiding citizens went in fear of their lives. There is no doubt the Scuttlers got a great thrill from the fear they induced in others. They thrived on the buzz of the chase and the high of an adrenaline rush. They regarded sweethearts as their property and used them as a means to demonstrate their hardness, usually when avenging slights, often entirely imaginary.

It was not only boys who followed this path. Mayhew encountered a prostitute of twelve and spoke at some length with one of sixteen. The latter was orphaned at an early age, and was sent into service at ten. Her life was so intolerable that she ran off after six months and found shelter in a lodging house. There she witnessed children of her own age sleeping with each other and before she was twelve she had taken up with a boy of fifteen.

For three years she plied her trade as a street walker, lodging in abject squalor in a house used by other prostitutes. She moved then to another house in which all the women were prostitutes, most controlled by pimps who beat them if they failed to bring home money and spent their days stealing, selling the proceeds in pubs or to the keeper of the house. The police, she contended, never called at such houses, though there was a constant stream of visitors, all thieves and prostitutes, many of whom bought a halfpenny worth of coffee, which entitled them to sit at the fire for as long as they chose.

Many of the waifs and strays who moved Dr Barnardo to set up his first children's home in 1870 lived in common lodging houses. One such was Mary B., a ten-year-old living a vagrant life with her father, who was described as 'a worthless fellow' and who, while living in a Surrey lodging house, was twice prosecuted for causing the girl to beg. Later he moved to another town where he was arrested and whereupon the magistrates decided to take the child from his care. She was subsequently accepted into one of Barnardo's homes.

Evangelical Christians also focused their attention on the lodging houses. These 'slum saviours' seldom met with a receptive audience and were likely to be dismissed as 'slummers'. Dr Barnardo, like many a slummer, was himself the object of prostitutes' ire when they accused him of luring away their men by encouraging them to lead useful lives.

Others sought to exploit the naivety of those seeking to reform them. The humiliation that befell a preacher from the Zion Chapel when he ventured into a notorious lodging house, the Phoenix, on the Ratcliffe Highway, was by no means unusual. He met there a cohabiting couple and encouraged them to sanctify their union in matrimony. In order to help them along, he provided the prospective bride with a separate room, a wedding dress and some furniture for the marital home. Immediately the groom pawned the dress and furniture and called off the wedding on the grounds that his proposed was already married to a sailor.

Despite the ire of many he hoped to reform and those who exploited them, Dr Barnardo persisted and opened his first home in 1866. The National Society for the Prevention of Cruelty to Children also helped to reduce the number of children who wandered about the country as aids to begging parents and unscrupulous adults. Other philanthropists who operated on a smaller scale, nevertheless provided practical help for children.

One such was John MacGregor, a barrister and ragged school teacher, who saw in the Great Exhibition of 1851 a wonderful opportunity to help the children of the streets: he employed 120 boys as shoe-blacks. The enterprise was so successful that the scheme provided the children with accommodation which thereby kept them away from the baleful influence of the lodging house and by 1877 provided honest employment for 385 boys.

It was from about this time that the number of children in lodging houses began to fall and by the early twentieth century the houses contained very few. Significantly, this also coincided with a fall in juvenile crime. There are many reasons for this shift, including the falling birth rate, the expansion of the Industrial School system, the growth of philanthropic societies catering specifically for children and the decline in seasonal jobs in agriculture because of increased mechanisation. The slowing rate at which towns grew in the second half of the nineteenth century also contributed to this downward trend.

Perhaps the most significant cause, however, was the development of compulsory education. At the beginning of the nineteenth century few poor children received regular weekday education, whereas from the 1870s most received some form of elementary education. The Education Act of 1870 was vital to this development, while the subsequent 1876 Act made attendance obligatory for those under ten.

What's more, from 1857 the courts had the power to deposit in industrial schools children aged between 7 and 14, who were deemed to be in danger of falling into a life of crime. In effect any child found begging or clearly lacking parental care was likely to end up in one of the schools, where he might be detained until he was 16. By 1898 there were over 22,000 children in these schools, most of whom would previously have crowded into low lodging houses and casual wards.

There was a difference between reformatories – where those convicted of serious offences were consigned – and industrial schools, where not all children were criminals; many in fact were the victims of neglect, as a result of which they were in danger of falling into crime. T.B.L. Baker, a Gloucester magistrate and an authority on juvenile crime, declared in the 1860s that the habitual, skilled boy-thief had ceased to exist outside London. He also discerned a reduction in crime in many large cities, such as Bristol, Birmingham and London. This he attributed to the practice of magistrates, from 1856, to routinely send second-time offenders to a reformatory. The effect of this in Gloucestershire was to reduce by half the number of juveniles appearing before the courts.

Similarly, the number of adults before the courts was also declining. The 1870s marked the beginning of a period of falling crime throughout the country which lasted until the end of the century. By the 1880s hundreds of juvenile criminals had already disappeared from the streets of major towns.

Yet as late as 1900 it was estimated that one in ten children were still working when they should have been in school. Ideally, Victorian children should have enjoyed the protection and nurture of a family, in the same way that the rightful place of a woman was thought to be at the centre of a home, supported by a husband. But just as many children were, in reality, forced to provide for themselves, there were many women who relied entirely on their own resources. When these proved inadequate many resorted to desperate measures.

Chapter Eight

Blowers and Blow-ins:
Fallen Women and Foreigners

Her screams, the long howls of a wounded beast demented with pain and rage, wakened the house. Doors opened and boots clattered on the stairs. When they saw her they shied in revulsion, covering their mouths in wide-eyed horror. She stood in a circle of blood, her face smeared and hair matted, her eyes wild with terror, her shift scarlet with only little cuffs of white unbloodied. The bed was sodden and drops of blood pulsed from the mattress and pooled on the floor.

We will never know exactly what occurred in cubicle 44 of William Crossingham's lodging house at 35 Dorset Street that night in May 1901. What is certain is that Mary Ann Austin, a 28-year-old prostitute, was subjected to a savage assault by a sadistic pervert, from which she died the following day.

Every evening the area to the east of Commercial Street, around Dorset Street, Whites Row and north of Pearl and Dean Street was awash with prostitutes. It was made infamous by the Jack the Ripper murders and most of his victims were women like Mary Ann who used the lodging houses around Flower and Dean Street as their base. Thirteen years before Mary Anne was murdered, Annie Chapman had left the same lodging house on the night she became a victim of the Ripper. It seemed that in the interim, despite the public outrage that followed the Ripper murders, little in the area had changed.

But brutal attacks on women were not confined to high-profile murders: they were part of the warp and weft of life in such areas. Shortly before the first Ripper murder hit the papers, a prostitute operating in the area had died as a result of a sadistic battering. Street gangs regarded prostitutes as fair game and seldom robbed them without also assaulting them, sometimes in the most obscene manner. In the slums a crude form of social Darwinism operated with tooth and claw savagery; old and broken prostitutes were at the bottom of the food chain.

The subsequent coroner's inquest and murder trial left the exact circumstances of Mary Anne's death a mystery. What they demonstrated clearly, however, was that the people of the slums lived in a hermetically sealed world in which the standards of the wider society were largely absent. The details of the case reveal that at the end of Victoria's reign the worst lodging houses remained as bad as they had ever been.

Purportedly a women's lodging house, William Crossingham's of 35 Dorset Street was known as a prostitutes' base. Mary Ann brought one of her clients there late on Saturday 25 May and paid the large sum of 1s 6d for a bed. The next morning, when her screams woke the house, there was no sign of the man. The keeper's wife, Maria Moore, sent for a doctor and summoned Daniel Sullivan – William Crossingham's brother-in-law and the keeper of another of his lodging houses. Sullivan immediately set about destroying all evidence of what had happened: he had Mary Ann's clothes burnt, washed and cleaned her and moved her to another bed.

Meanwhile the doctor arrived and recognising that her condition was perilous, sent Mary-Ann to hospital, where she died the next day. It was only then that the police became aware of what had happened. Their attempts to discover the circumstances surrounding Mary Ann's death proved futile: all the witnesses lied and when their lies were exposed they merely told a fresh set of lies. Their accounts were riddled with inconsistencies and contradictions.

The man who had gone to bed with Mary Ann claimed to be her husband and swore that when he left her she was perfectly well; there was nothing in the testimony of the witnesses to suggest otherwise. The judge had insufficient evidence to convict anyone. The *Daily Mail* fulminated against all the usual suspects, blaming the keepers and describing the Dorset Street lodging houses as 'the head centre of the shifting criminal population of London … the common thief, the area sneak, the man who robs with violence and the unconvicted murderer'. Nor were the police blameless: they 'have a theory that it is better to let these people congregate together in one mass where they can be easily found than to scatter them abroad.'

The Victorians believed that the lodging house was inextricably linked with prostitution. Few writers on one failed to mention the other. It was widely believed that they were the means by which many innocent country girls, newly arrived in the city, were induced into a life of vice. Contemporary observers invariably concluded that there was a close link between living conditions and sexual licence generally. This was a leitmotif running through every discussion on housing and social conditions. As one commentator put it, 'The greatest immorality is the necessary result of their promiscuously crowded habitations.' Nowhere was overcrowding more evident than in the lodging house.

Public concern with prostitution suggests that it was a widespread problem and that it was the major route by which women passed beyond the realms of respectability. In fact, there were significant numbers of women, apart from prostitutes, who existed beyond the social pale. Women made up one in four of the vagrants arrested by the Metropolitan Police in the decade up to 1843 and in the 1860s they constituted between one-third and a quarter of known tramps. Throughout the period their numbers declined relative to those of men and by the end of the nineteenth century there were nine male tramps for every female.

Nevertheless in the 1870s and 1880s women made up between a fifth and a third of the occupants of lodging houses. Women's beds in lodging houses were generally more expensive than men's. Mary Higgs' experience of such places at the end of the nineteenth century led her to believe that many of the women who used them were prostitutes who spent most of the evening dressing, went out at 10pm and generally returned drunk. She also maintained that the shortage of single beds for women forced them to take a man into the double bed with them in order to cover the cost. Many of the girls who worked in the lodging houses were, Higgs believed, coerced into prostitution by the keepers, who in effect became their pimps.

In 1901 over four million women, almost a third of the entire female population, were engaged in industrial or domestic employment. Like her male equivalent, the unemployed woman often had to travel in search of work. In practice few respectable women travelled alone, as it was generally assumed that a woman living on her own in particular lodging houses was a prostitute.

Then, as now, it was extremely difficult to determine the number of prostitutes operating at any one time. Estimates vary wildly. In 1851 William Acton calculated that there were 210,000 prostitutes in London alone – a figure equal to half the number of unmarried women in the city. A decade earlier the Commissioner of the Metropolitan Police put the number of street walkers at 7,000, excluding the City of London area. Writing in 1857, Dr Michael Ryan, an authority on such matters, claimed that there were 80,000 professional whores in the capital and that they made something in the order of £8 million a year.

Though Acton's figure is undoubtedly an overestimate, most commentators agree that police estimates are on the low side and put the figure at about 55,000 in mid-nineteenth century London. Data from provincial cities and towns suggest similarly high numbers. In 1843 the Manchester police calculated that there were 330 brothels and 701 'common prostitutes' in the city. This figure, however, like all police estimates, is certainly on the low side, as it includes only prostitutes known to them. The Chief Constable, Captain Palin, stated in his report for 1868 that there were 981 convictions of prostitutes for being drunk and disorderly and only 92 for accosting wayfarers. There were at that time 'over 800 prostitutes in the city and 325 houses of ill-fame', which almost certainly refers to houses, often lodging houses, used by prostitutes, as well as brothels. Nearly all of these women, in common with all the prostitutes who came to the attention of the police, combined theft with selling their bodies.

One reason why estimates are problematic is because of changes in the way prostitutes operated. From the 1830s to the 1850s the number of brothels declined, while the number of prostitutes operating on their own account remained constant. Police identified almost 2,000 London houses where prostitutes lodged in 1857 and the same number a decade later. However, these figures do not include occasional prostitutes.

Prostitutes – also known as 'gay', 'mott' and 'blowers' – were found in certain districts of most cities and towns, often the same areas in which lodging houses were concentrated. Figures produced by the Metropolitan Police District for 1857 list these areas as: Spitalfields, Whitechapel, Ratcliff, Bethnal Green, Mile End, Lambeth, Southwark, Bermondsey, Rotherhithe, Westminster and Marylebone.

Regardless of where they operated, prostitutes used a range of similar strategies to alert potential customers to their availability. The most blatant signal was to walk the street without a hat or a shawl – thus violating taboos against a woman displaying her hair or figure in public. To make it even more obvious she would parade up and down the same stretch of pavement in a languorous manner, while looking about her, as no respectable woman dawdled in the street. By turning around to make eye contact with a man and then pursing her lips to make a suggestive sound a woman announced her trade.

Often it was unnecessary for her to do any of these things; certain areas and streets in cities and towns were so powerfully associated with prostitution that any woman standing about there was immediately deemed to be soliciting. Particular venues – public houses, theatres and music halls, pleasure gardens and the streets around railway stations and docks – were the prostitute's natural habitat. In the nineteenth century the capital's sex trade became an inextricable part of the West End. Prostitutes colonised it area by area – Covent Garden, Haymarket and then Piccadilly.

By the 1850s there were so many prostitutes on the streets of London that competition was fierce and disputes over territory often vitriolic. Though modern commentators are inclined to sentimentalise the nature of prostitutes' relationship with each other, sometimes suggesting a sisterhood bound together by shared suffering and the need for mutual support, the reality is far less edifying. Women were more often engaged in violent antagonism against those they saw as threatening their 'pitch' and thereby their livelihood, than in offering succour to fellow unfortunates. Many contemporaries explained these women's violent behaviour towards each other as the inevitable result of their moral degeneracy and love of drink. Often, however, their battles were motivated by cold calculation of what was necessary to protect their interests; like all entrepreneurs they sought to deter rivals threatening their business.

A major threat to their trade was the Criminal Law Amendment Act of 1885 which made it an offence to procure a woman for immoral purposes, thus giving the police powers to prosecute brothel-keepers. In the wake of the legislation brothels and lodging houses used as houses of ill repute were closed in enormous numbers and parallel measures against street soliciting forced the women to adopt a far less blatant approach. To add to their problems, the new regime forced many women to rent a room from which to operate. Alone in a room or a house without the support of other prostitutes, women were vulnerable to attack. Only a minority of prostitutes operated from enclosed brothels and these women tended to be of the more exalted type. In London, for instance, the number of reported brothels declined from 933 to 410 in the 36 years after 1841.

During the same period licensing laws were also refined, with the result that the landlords of pubs faced far harsher penalties for renting rooms to prostitutes. The result was that increasingly the common prostitute who infested the slums of most urban areas lived in a lodging house.

Given the squalid and dangerous life of a prostitute, commentators were at a loss to explain why so many women were drawn to it. By the mid-eighteenth century it was common for popular writers to promote the fiction that prostitutes were generally naive country girls corrupted by cynical roués or calculating lodging house keepers. Prostitutes were known, in polite society, as 'unfortunates'. Many blamed drink, just as today it is fashionable to attribute much crime to drug abuse. Current research, however, suggests that the modern malefactor is a criminal first and an addict second and that criminality is a far better predictor of addiction than addiction of criminality. Victorians assumed that drink was a major factor in the decline of women into prostitution, though it is equally possible that many women were prostitutes before they became drunkards.

Certainly, many prostitutes, especially those past their best, were alcoholics, often partial to White Satin, which was popular with those for whom gin was a favourite tipple. These women did not confine their drinking to public houses. Mary Higgs was clearly disgusted when she came across a group of such women drinking during the day in one of the women's lodging houses she visited in 1901. Prostitution was so widespread in certain quarters that it was accepted as part of the natural order of things. One Victorian authority on prostitution, William Acton, expressed his surprise that in the East End of London prostitutes often plied their trade in public houses where respectable women were also to be found with their husbands.

Prostitutes solicited in most places where working men drank, particularly the gin palace. It is difficult for us to appreciate the appeal of the gin palace to the Victorians. The labouring man's working conditions were always harsh and functional and living conditions invariably little better. With a cold stone floor and perhaps nothing more than a rag rug and a few ornaments to soften the grim practicality of his home, the gin palace had an alluring bright glow, its plate glass, polished mirrors, burnished mahogany bar and opulent chandeliers irresistible to those who craved some luxury in their lives. It was one of the few places the poor experienced which exuded opulence and helped them forget the scrimping that was at the centre of working class life.

It is also impossible to discuss prostitutes without discussing money. As one author put it, prostitution offered 'rich rewards and considerable incentives compared with twelve hour days losing their eyesight sewing shirts in a sweatshop or scrubbing floors'. Presumably the author was thinking of the upmarket prostitute who drew her clients from the wealthy.

The most fortunate of these was the 'kept woman', set up in a substantial house in the suburbs by a well-heeled lover. Among prostitutes, as among all those who live beyond the purview of respectability, there was a hierarchy of esteem. At the lower echelons were most of the prostitutes who appeared daily before the courts and those such as the victims of Jack the Ripper who lived a precarious existence on the periphery of destitution, their lives unrelieved by any hint of luxury.

On this matter, as on so many other aspects of the life of the Victorian poor, Mayhew offers invaluable insight. He divides prostitutes into six categories. At the bottom of the pile were what Mayhew describes as 'thieves' women'. These were women who were normally financially dependent on professional criminals with neither a history nor any intention of working. When the thief in their life was in prison they prostituted themselves.

Next came 'park women', prostitutes unable or unwilling to take clients indoors who instead offered their services in public spaces, not only in parks but in back alleys and doorways. The amount they earned was minuscule and their standard of living truly wretched. These were the base of the pyramid, 'low prostitutes' who infested the poorest neighbourhoods and, at the weekend, the city centre. They sold themselves to the first man they could entice and generally knew no other trade, lacking any experience of prolonged work.

Slightly above were the women who regarded prostitution as a stopgap measure, a means of feeding themselves when times were bad. When there was an upturn in trade they went back to making a living by honest labour. The mill girls who thronged Manchester city centre in times of slack trade fell into this category.

Next came 'sailors' and soldiers' women'. Sailors were a major source of income for prostitutes, who were always to be found in large numbers around docks. Sailors' women – nicknamed 'leggers' motts' – were a feature of all ports. Mayhew observed that many sailors, instead of availing themselves of several prostitutes, took up with a particular one who, while he was ashore, acted as his wife. Many of these women, he noticed, were foreigners. The appeal of sailors, once renowned for their extravagance, declined sharply towards the end of the nineteenth century when measures were implemented to encourage them to save a share of their wages, thereby putting it beyond the grasping whores and scheming landlords for whom every ship that docked held out the promise of rich pickings.

Only after these groups do we reach the women of the 'low lodging houses'. There is some evidence that former prostitutes frequently set themselves up as madams running brothels or as keepers of low lodging houses. Mayhew's research in the 1850s led him to conclude that it was common for boys and men to pick up women in the street and take them back to a lodging house. Many of these houses were to all intents and purposes brothels, with women coming and going throughout the night. The majority of houses described as brothels in police returns were lodging houses where prostitutes took their clients. Most catered for casual prostitutes who picked up men in pubs, music halls and pleasure gardens. The police attitude to these establishments was generally tolerant, provided they gave rise to few complaints of violence and robbery.

Investigations into lodging houses in Cardiff just before the First World War found that many of their keepers were living with – if not on the earnings of – women to whom they were not married. At the same time Mary Higgs was convinced that women who left their homes to become lodgers – often young girls in search of work or accommodation – frequently resorted to prostitution when they fell on hard times. This, Higgs believed, was a major reason why so few respectable women resorted to lodging houses as they believed that to do so risked being drawn into prostitution. The figures for 15 January 1909 for London suggest that women did generally avoid lodging houses: on that night there were 1,483 women and 161 children in common lodging houses, compared with 20,059 men. In casual wards there were 184 women, 3 children and 1,903 men.

As late as 1909 Mary Higgs maintained that many girls who originally came to work in lodging houses were drawn into prostitution. These prostitutes' lodging houses were commonly regarded as just as pernicious and corrupting as prostitution itself. The prostitutes slopped about during the day, squatting in front of the kitchen fire, gossiping and generally, in the opinion of one observer, 'eroding all decency, modesty, propriety and conscience'.

Areas such as Spitalfields, with numerous common lodging houses, were also full of tenements where rooms were let by the week and frequently occupied by one or more families. These, even more than the common lodging houses, were favoured by prostitutes as both a base and a place to take clients. But they continued to use lodging houses because, as the *East London Observer* bemoaned in 1888, 'a woman is at perfect liberty to bring any companion she likes to share her accommodation'.

In mid-nineteenth century London prostitutes, including those based in lodging houses, were generally controlled by women. Many of the keepers of lodging houses used by prostitutes were themselves former prostitutes. They took a share of their charges' earnings, in return for which they provided security against those clients who might seek to beat them up. Male pimps – other than those who were in a long-term sexual relationship with prostitutes – were virtually unheard of at this time. One of the effects of the Ripper murders of 1888 was that prostitutes sought the protection of male pimps, many of whom were career criminals well practised in extreme violence. Prior to this prostitution was run and controlled by women.

Even women who took a bully protector were sometimes victims of violence. However, prostitutes were not always the blameless victims: when violence occurred, it was often in the course of a prostitute trying to rob her client. By their nature the areas prostitutes worked were the most violent parts of the city.

The area around Dorset Street is a case in point. It was attractive to prostitutes not simply because of the number of rooms let by the week. The market offered many workers and traders who were away from home; the docks provided a constant supply of sailors; the West End was nearby and Spitalfields was irresistible to gentlemen who craved the frisson of 'slumming it'. The women who operated in such areas made up the great bulk of the city's prostitutes and attracted the attention of police and commentators.

Even among these, however, the ones who ended up in court were the dregs – drunkards who assaulted and robbed their clients, loudmouthed, dirty harridans who harassed pedestrians and gave the police no choice but to arrest them. In other ways these were the most vulnerable. Often semi-professional whores who had neither pimp nor protector and living in lodging houses without a husband, they were at the mercy of the sadist and the sexual murderer. It was from this group that Jack the Ripper chose his victims.

The Ripper, however, was only the most infamous murderer of prostitutes. Thomas Neil Cream, having been convicted of murder in Canada, arrived in Britain in 1891 and immediately targeted prostitutes. Within a year he poisoned four of them before Lou Harvey, an intended victim, recognised him and alerted the police.

The top two categories of prostitutes occupied a totally different realm from their unfortunate sisters and lived an altogether better life. The larger group was what Mayhew called 'the convives', known today as 'escorts'. Some were independent, working out of their own accommodation, finding their own clients and occasionally managing to snare a wealthy husband. Others were subject to a mistress or madam who provided board and often clothes for her charges. In addition the mistress provided clients. In other cases the women sallied forth, returning with their own clients.

Either way the dangers and discomforts of their situation were beyond anything experienced by the 'kept mistress' who occupied the pinnacle of the fallen woman's aspirations. She was the prima donna of whoredom, the acme of the profession. To all impressions she lived like a woman of independent means and lacked nothing that an indulgent and affluent lover might provide. Very often such women succeeded by wise marriage to wheedle their way into respectable society where, as paragons of propriety, they lived in dread of their colourful past coming to light. A woman of this type is the subject of William Holman Hunt's *The Awakening Conscious*.

The kept woman was by no means typical and it was the prevalence of hordes of low prostitutes in certain prominent areas of Britain's cities and towns that prompted attempts to eradicate what many regarded as a national scandal. In London, the Metropolitan Police Act of 1850 made 'loitering' an offence, while from 1858 any premises harbouring more than a single prostitute was deemed a brothel, rendering the landlord liable to prosecution. It also became an offence for publicans to allow their premises to become places where prostitutes gathered.

In particular, the threat to the health of soldiers and sailors posed by their use of prostitutes led to the Contagious Diseases Act of 1864. This meant that any woman accused of prostitution by the police could be forcibly medically examined. Should she refuse, she could be consigned to a Lock Hospital, which specialised in the treatment of venereal disease, where she might be detained indefinitely.

Prostitution was not confined to women. Male prostitutes – known as 'sods', 'margeries' and 'poofs' – were conspicuous in Fleet Street and the Strand in the 1850s and there were streets and bars in most large cities and towns where they were to be found. Like prostitution, the 'abominable crime of buggery' was a criminal offence carrying a penalty of two years' imprisonment. Many of the boys with whom Oscar Wilde and his coterie consorted were children who lived in common lodging houses and had neither regular employment nor settled abode.

Immigrants and the Lodging House

Britain, it is said, has always provided a welcome for those who leave home in search of a better life. It is nearer the truth, however, to say that the rookeries and the slums have provided the welcome: only affluent immigrants settle in the leafy suburbs and most immigrants are far from affluent. Newly arrived immigrants were one of the largest groups drawn to the lodging houses. Throughout the nineteenth century there was an unbroken flow of newcomers to these shores and they had a significant impact on the life of the lodging houses.

As early as 1500, there were 3,000 foreigners in London, then about 6 per cent of the population. A couple of centuries later the coronation of the first German king, George I – George Louis, Elector of Hanover – in 1714, planted his entourage at the centre of British public life but it was only in the early years of Victoria's reign that Britain became particularly attractive to the poor and the persecuted. The emancipation of first Catholics and then Jews made the country a haven of liberty at a time when industry's demand for cheap labour was insatiable.

By 1871 Germans comprised one of Britain's largest foreign-born minorities. Many were in the food trade – especially butchery – and popularised the traditional British breakfast of bacon and sausage. A significant percentage of these German immigrants were Jews and, despite their penetration of the apex of society, the East End of London was still home to most Jews, even as the affluent were moving to the suburbs of Ilford, Redbridge and Finchley. Most, however, remained poor, eking out a living in the second-hand clothes trade or tramping the country as peddlers. Soon there were significant Jewish communities in Manchester and Leeds.

Just as the Jews were associated with street trading, the Italians were often street entertainers. Most members of the nineteenth century Italian community remained in London – so many lived in the area around Hatton Garden and Little Saffron Hill in Clerkenwell that it was known as 'Little Italy'. By 1901 the number of Italian-born in Britain topped 25,000 and there were sizeable communities in Manchester, Liverpool, Newcastle, Sheffield, Bradford, Leeds and Hull. Most were involved in the retail food business – as chefs, bakers and cafe owners or selling chestnuts and, of course, ice cream. The Scots in particular were great fans and by 1911 Glasgow boasted 300 ice-cream parlours.

As late as 1892, Thomas Wright, writing of the area around the port of London, describes a lodging house for foreign organ grinders with a storage area for their organs and another for all variety of street musicians, including the lowly ballad singer who was at the bottom of this particular hierarchy. 'Musician' was an occupation commonly found on census returns for those living in lodging houses. Adding to the diversions were the Punch and Judy men, the walking dogs and tamed bears, the mobile peep shows, the pipers, fiddlers, squeeze-box players, flautists, harpers – often with accompanying dancers – and the ubiquitous organ grinders, with their deep and penetrating music an irresistible magnet for children and street Arabs of all hues.

By the 1850s Italian organ grinders were part of the furniture of the streets. In Manchester Germans and other foreigners tended to gather in a few lodgings where they could spend time with their countrymen. By all accounts their houses, and the ones favoured by Italian organ grinders, were far cleaner and altogether better than the norm. When Joseph Johnson, a local journalist, described the horrors of Manchester's lodging houses in the mid-nineteenth century, he excepted the one used by Germans, describing it as clean, homely and 'full of good-natured foreigners'. The Italian house in Edge Street was also excellent.

Conspicuous as the Italians were, their numbers were insignificant in comparison with the Irish. While the Mediterranean immigrants brought a splash of exoticism to Britain's drab industrial cities, those from across the Irish Sea were seen as enemies who made the hard life of the indigenous poor even harder. Many influential commentators blamed the Irish for urban squalor and found in them an outlet for the anti-Catholic bigotry endemic in nineteenth century Britain. The eminent historian James Froude described the Irish as more akin to apes than humans and Thomas Carlisle dismissed them as spreaders of squalor and chaos. The *Manchester City News* of 12 March 1864 found there were 472 lodging houses in the city; of these 147 were the resort of known thieves, 244 were occupied by vagrants and 'poor travellers' and 72 by hawkers, foreigners and the Irish.

Those Irish who arrived as the Famine began to cut great swathes through the population were often destitute: between 1846 and 1848 almost 16,000 of those admitted to the Asylum for the Houseless Poor in Playhouse Yard, Cripplegate were newly arrived Irish. Even greater numbers arrived in Liverpool. Of those who arrived there in 1848, 161,000 were paupers, half-naked and starving, who threw themselves immediately on the mercy of the parish. Newport was also flooded by desperate arrivals. The Irish, both those who intended to stay and those hoping to go to America, also arrived in Bristol and Scotland in large numbers. The roads from Bristol to London thronged with immigrants.

Irish lodging houses, in common with those urban slums where they lived in great numbers, had a vile reputation. Mayhew's informants in the 1850s told him that 'the Irish will sleep anywhere to save a halfpenny at night if they have ever so much money'. It was widely assumed that every Irish lodging house had its own poteen still and that inmates existed in a state of perpetual drunkenness. In 1836, for instance, the Manchester police found that 'illicit spirits were often clandestinely sold in them and hawked about by Irish women'. Many of them were 'crammed with Irish the whole of Saturday night and parties of men came mad-drunk out of these places.'

A high proportion of foreigners also found their way to lodging houses in rural areas where there was a demand for seasonal labour. In mid-nineteenth century, for instance, eleven per cent of lodgers in the St Thomas' area of Oxford were Irish and five per cent European. Far more than the indigenous population, the Irish had a penchant for lodgings: in 1851 about a third of Irishmen between 20 and 44 years of age lived in lodgings of some type. The Irish therefore comprised a substantial proportion of lodgers and also of owners and keepers. In St Thomas', Oxford, certain lodging houses became a focal point for the Irish arriving in the city. There was also one that was favoured by German and Italian musicians who were as much a feature of town life as they were of the cities.

As late as the 1860s the *Manchester Guardian* was still reminding its readers of the Irish peril after its reporter visited a lodging house on Charter Street, in Angel Meadow. As expected, he encountered all the shocking details he sought. Lodgers needed only 3*d* for a bed for the night, very often sleeping in buildings which had previously been pubs but had lost their licences. The pub landlord was now the landlord of the lodging house, often with the same clients. Some landlords displayed remarkable ingenuity in their efforts to maximise profits. One even removed the roof to cram in more lodgers.

It is hardly surprising that the great influx of Jews escaping persecution in the final three decades of the nineteenth century should receive a lukewarm welcome. As well as renewed pogroms in Russia and Eastern Europe, a cholera epidemic in Poland and famine in Lithuania caused many to flee. In 1886 Jews were expelled from northern Germany and from Moscow in 1890. In 1900 3,000 redoubtable souls crossed Europe on foot in order to get to England.

Many arrived on the south coast destitute. The 150,000 immigrants who settled in Britain between 1881 and 1914 soon overwhelmed the Board of Guardians for the Relief of the Jewish Poor. The newcomers huddled together behind the docks in London, in the Leylands of Leeds and in Strangeways, Manchester. In 1889 the Jews of Kottingen in Lithuania decamped en masse to Sunderland.

But nowhere was the Jewish presence more evident than in London's East End. The earliest Jewish immigrants got a toehold in the second-hand clothes trade and soon dominated the markets at Houndsditch and Petticoat Lane. Those who came after them developed a network of tailoring shops which undercut the competition and produced clothes at prices lower than anyone thought possible.

Jews also specialised in cabinet- and shoe-making and these trades formed the basis of the success of smaller communities in Liverpool, Glasgow, Birmingham, Hull and Newcastle. As in London, most of the Manchester Jews found work in the cheap clothing and household furniture trades, centred on Red Bank, Strangeways and Lower Broughton, where there was plenty of inexpensive housing, many lodging houses and a long-standing reputation for crime and disorder. Like the Irish, the Jews attracted hostility from their hosts yet by 1914 there were 300,000 Jews in Britain.

One of the many concerns raised by this influx was that it coincided with a significant increase in crime and many commentators linked this to urbanisation and mass immigration. John Wade spelled out this connection when he contrasted the small towns, from which so many immigrants originated, consisting of a settled population, on the one hand, and great cities, on the other, where many of the inhabitants were migratory. In the former, 'the retreats and opportunities for delinquency are few and limited; the pursuits and even the character of each person are matters of notoriety and interest; not to be known is to be an object of inquiry and suspicion: in a word, everyone is the police of his neighbour, and unconsciously exercises over him its most essential duties.' No one who has ever lived in a village or small town could doubt that Wade has put his finger on the social value of what many people resent as the intrusive nosiness of neighbours who seem obsessed with the minutiae of others' lives.

In the cities 'there is no curiosity about neighbours – everyone is engrossed in his own pursuits and neither knows nor cares about any human being except the circle to which he has been introduced and to which he is connected by ties of business, pleasure or profit.' This is the city so many experience today, where no one knows their neighbours and people lie dead in their homes undiscovered for months, because people 'don't like to interfere'. It is because of this, Wade adds that 'cities afford so many facilities for the concealment of criminality ... The metropolis is like an immense forest in the innumerable avenues of which offenders may always find retreat and shelter.'

One result of this widespread fear of crime with which immigrants were linked was legislation which fundamentally altered the status of those wishing to settle in Britain. By the 1905 Aliens Act entry to Britain was no longer a right. Anyone who could not support himself could now be sent back to his country of origin. However, a number of recent immigrants had already found a very lucrative way of supporting themselves and were yet regarded as a far greater threat to society than anyone who had been prevented from entering the country.

Chapter Nine

Ferdinando Ferina and the Man Who Spits Fire and Glass: The Lodging House Owner and Keeper

'God curse you bastards to hell,' he wailed, his great sweating bulk filling the doorway. 'Come one step nearer,' he said, brandishing the metal leg of a bed above his greasy head, 'and I'll split ye.' He steadied himself with his left hand against the flaking jamb of the door and moved his head from side to side like a tormented hound sniffing the air. His eyelids flickered like a wayward pulse over his blind eyes, one pointing east and the other west.

'Now Con,' said the emollient policeman, 'that's no way to greet this gentleman who's come here special to see you.'

'That's right, sir,' said James Greenwood, taking half a pace forward yet remaining beyond the orbit of the bed leg. Even from that distance he could smell his host's potent mixture of sweat and alcohol; it was as if alcohol were seeping from his clammy skin. 'Delighted to make your acquaintance, sir,' said Greenwood, extending his hand and then letting it fall to his side.

In 1874 James Greenwood visited the lodging houses of Golden Lane, in the City, and on meeting the proprietor of one he was not disappointed. Every negative expectation he brought to the encounter was confirmed by Blind Con, famed for his antipathy to all officials. Con was the perfect caricature of the lodging house owner: a violent, villainous rogue who encouraged and gained from the criminality of his lodgers.

But what do we know about other lodging house owners and how far does this confirm the negative stereotype?

Owners were, of course, of various different types. Many were speculative builders but most began by purchasing an old building. A typically shrewd entrepreneur, who realised that the rising demand for cheap accommodation represented a major opportunity for those with a relatively small amount to invest, was John Miller. When the demolition that prepared the way for the Commercial Road development of 1845 reduced the number of beds in the area, Miller was a butcher with premises at 30 Dorset Street. He immediately bought 26 and 27 in the same street. The buildings were adjacent to each other and came with large gardens accessible from the street and in which he eventually built six cottages; this became Miller's Court, where the horribly mutilated body of Mary Kelly, the Ripper's final victim, was discovered.

The houses at 26 and 27 Dorset Street were converted in the same manner in which countless similar old buildings were made ready for service as lodging houses. Each floor was gutted and made into a large dormitory, while the ground floor was converted into a communal kitchen to serve both houses. The other floors were packed with cheap beds, usually with straw-filled mattresses.

Most of the lodging houses in the area made infamous by the Ripper murders were owned by Frederick Gehringer, Jimmy Smith and his sister Elizabeth and Daniel Lewis and his sons. Smith and Gehringer also owned several pubs in the area. The lodging houses in Dorset Street were the fiefdom of Jack McCarthy and his friend and business associate, William Crossingham. Smith and McCarthy took a keen interest in prize-fighting and organised a number of bouts, offering facilities for sporting gentlemen to wager a few pounds on their fancy. Despite their nefarious activities and reputation as men who could look after themselves, their lodging houses provided an invaluable service for those who would not countenance the workhouse.

They also provided a range of additional services for their niche clientele. McCarhy and Smith owned 'open all hours' general stores near their houses which stocked everything a lodger might want. Among their pubs on Dorset Street alone they owned the gargantuan Britannia, the Blue Coat Bay and the Horn of Plenty, which, even by the standards of the area was no place for the drinker who had led a sheltered life. The building next to the Britannia was a brothel, where two spinsters made under-age girls available to their clients.

Other owners in the Spitalfields area were of a similar background to Miller. John Smith started out as a greengrocer and gradually acquired properties around Brick Lane until, by the 1860s, lodging houses were his main concern. Three of his children followed in his footsteps and became well-known keepers in the area.

The investments of Miller and Smith appeared prescient by the late 1840s, when an influx of Famine Irish created an insatiable demand for cheap accommodation. By 1849 there were 50,000 Famine Irish in London desperate for a place to lay their heads. The Irish soon became synonymous with the poorest peddlers, selling oranges, fish, cress, matches and vegetables – all areas in which, because of their ability to live on the meanest pittance, they were able to undercut their rivals. Others worked as unskilled labour in the building trade and when all else failed, begged.

The value of houses in Dorset Street area decreased in relation to the number of lodging houses in the area. At the same time their owners were less inclined to waste money on a depreciating asset. The death of a child in 1857, when part of a dilapidated house in Dorset Street crushed him to death, indicated what was already well-known: most of the houses in the street and many in the wider area were unsound and therefore worth little on the open market, so consequently could be bought cheaply. Many of the new landlords in this area were men whose money had been acquired by dishonest means, often gamblers or thieves according to Mayhew. Others raised the money by selling shares. Adverts in local newspapers, assuring investors of an annual return of four per cent, were common throughout most of the nineteenth century.

The link between alcohol and lodging houses was common in the cities and towns. Writing of Bethnal Green in 1848, Hector Gavin found that 'nearly all the small public houses and beershops take in lodgers'. The Beer Act of 1830 in effect made it possible for virtually anyone to set up a 'beerhouse' which offered beers and ales at reasonable prices. Many having attracted a crowd by luring them with an evening's entertainment, saw no reason to send them home: why not also provide them with accommodation? About one in every fifteen lodging houses in towns was also a beershop, while the fraction in the country was far greater.

In many ways a lodging house was an ideal investment for the craftsman fortunate enough to have an industrious and forceful wife to run the business while he continued his trade. An analysis of the lodging houses in St Thomas', Oxford, shows that of the heads of households which were lodging houses only fifteen per cent described themselves as 'lodging house keepers', while the remainder worked in commerce and industry. A third of all heads of households were in trades closely associated with lodging houses, such as licensed victuallers, innkeepers, publicans and beerhouse keepers. By far the most frequent occupation of owners was that of keeper of a beerhouse which accounted for about one in every fifteen in London and as many as one in four in other areas. The remainder worked in jobs that were common in the area where they lived and seven per cent were general labourers.

A study of 330 common lodging houses based on the 1861 census suggests that, though eighty per cent were owned by men, many were managed by owners' wives or other family members. In London, however, there were more women than men owners. Less than one in ten of male keepers were single, whereas nearly eighty per cent of the women were widowed or unmarried. Owning and running a lodging house was also seen as a good way for a single woman to make a living.

It was also a means by which men of humble origins and modest means could rise in the world. Thomas Wright, discussing lodging houses around the port of London in 1892, confirms this: 'Many of them are the property and most of them are under the management of one speculator in this line of business. This man may fairly claim to rank among "men who have risen" or be classed with the "self-made".' Many of these, he believed, arrived in the capital and were indistinguishable from the penniless throng of newcomers in search of work until they began assisting the manager of a lodging house, before developing the necessary skills and advancing to acquiring their own property.

Both Mayhew and Charles Booth agreed with Wright that the owners of the most basic lodging houses were very much like their lodgers. Mayhew claimed that eighty per cent of them had once been travellers and analysis of census returns suggests that there was certainly a great deal of common experience between the two groups. A few examples will suffice to support this view.

The keepers of houses in Hereford in 1861, for instance, included nine publicans, three general labourers, two hawkers, two farm labourers, a copper smith, a nailer, a tinplate worker, a shoe-maker, a tailor, a servant, a gloveress, a horse-keeper and a seedsman. Oxford's keepers in the same year comprised a street sweeper, a boot-maker, a laundress, a journeyman bookbinder, a stonemason, a coachman, a baker, a plasterer and a bricklayer, while Leicester's included a dealer in clothes, a firewood-seller, a hawker of small wares, a bricklayer's labourer, a coal heaver, a maker of umbrellas, a night soil man, several agricultural labourers and a framework knitter. A house in Market Deeping was kept by a married couple who described themselves as 'travellers'.

The censuses abound with examples, such as that of 1851 for Stamford in Lincolnshire, a town with a population of just over 9,000. At that time there were twenty-nine lodging houses there, two of which belonged to John McCormick, a hawker and Thomas McSweeney, an agricultural labourer. Another owner, John Farnell was, like McCormick and McSweeney, Irish and those lodging in all three houses were predominantly Irishmen. This is yet another way in which keepers resembled their lodgers.

In many Surrey lodging houses during the second half of the nineteenth century it was not uncommon to find two or more houses owned by the same family. Keeping a lodging house was often a family business. At the lowest level many people opened up their homes as lodging houses as a means of keeping a roof over their head.

The average lodging house in a county town had room for between eight and ten lodgers and it is estimated that a house with six lodgers could generate an income of no more than 14s a week, sufficient to provide a pinched standard of living. Consequently, in most cases owners generally had another source of income and it was usual for a wife to manage the lodging house while her husband pursued his chief occupation.

There is no doubt that women played a major role in the functioning of lodging houses, not just as managers but also as owners. Of the 1,401 lodging houses listed in the London post office directory in 1851 half were owned by women. Of those listed in a survey of lodging houses in market towns in central England in 1851, nearly nine out of every ten keepers were female. For many middle class women, especially those from the lower middle class, economic necessity compelled them to make a living and a lodging house provided one of a limited number of options. It was common for a spinster or a widow to team up with another woman in a joint venture.

A study of lodging house owners and keepers in Hastings during the period 1839 to 1851 shows that many were women. Those of the better houses often described themselves as 'blooming widows'. But ownership also afforded opportunities for the enterprising slum dweller. One such was Susan Morgan, a second-hand clothes dealer in the Nichol, an infamous rookery in the East End, who ran a lodging house next to a pub in Turk Street.

In Chester many of the owners and keepers were widows or women abandoned by husbands and left with children to support. A study of owners and keepers in Leicester found that many were elderly widows, often suffering from downward social mobility, which forced them to use their homes as a source of income.

Mayhew's claim that about half of London's mid-nineteenth century owners had once been travellers may be suggestive of the situation in the capital but is not supported by evidence from other parts of the country. Analysis of the data from St Thomas', Oxford, suggests that seventy per cent of owners were born in the area, though a significant number were foreigners, including some colourful characters who had lived exciting lives.

One of these, the wonderfully named Ferdinando Ferina, was said to have walked to England from southern Italy before establishing a lodging house dynasty in the city. Not content with housing a large portion of the local drifters, he also wanted to fill the city's streets with the sound of music: he rented out barrel–organs. His wife was renowned as a good woman: she tended the ailments of her most unfortunate lodgers. Other unusual characters associated with the city's lodging houses included a Negro bouncer who, having tired of chewing glass and eating fire for a living, ran away from the circus and supported himself by maintaining order in one of the city's lodging houses and another Italian family, whose accommodation was markedly inferior to that of the compassionate Mrs Ferina and was well-known for being 'dirty, damp and dilapidated'.

One of the great attractions of a lodging house was that start–up costs were low. All that was needed was the capital to acquire a lease on a suitable property, which Mayhew believed could be had for as little as 8s a week and certainly no more than 20s. It was easy to furnish it with items that were virtually unsaleable: one keeper Mayhew cites, less pernickety than his competitors, bought his furniture from a smallpox hospital and others from cholera hospitals. Thereafter the chief running costs were gas and coal.

Charging no more than a few pence per night, was it possible for the owner to make a profit? The unanimous answer of all those with personal experience of such places and all the commentators is a resounding affirmative.

Mayhew estimated that, on average, large London lodging houses took about 17s 6d a night. Others, usually of the most disreputable sort, made a great deal more. A Mrs Cummins of St Giles is said to have charged her clients between 1s 6d and 2s per hour. The owner of six houses in and around Thrawl Street in Whitechapel never went near the East End but luxuriated in the splendour of his palatial home in Hampstead.

One of Mayhew's 1850 informants told him that quite apart from it being common for one person to own as many as ten lodging houses, a single house accommodating eighty men produced a profit of £500 a year. Given that anyone earning £150, such as a senior clerk, was regarded as middle class, this is equivalent to a professional's salary. This remained the situation throughout the nineteenth century. Talking in 1853 of what he regarded as one of the worst rookeries in London, St James's, peopled by thieves and beggars, the City Missionary, Mr Walker, was convinced that the owners of lodging houses in such areas made a great deal of money.

Referring specifically to Flower and Dean Street in the 1880s, J.E. Ritchie believed that, despite all the regulation, it was still possible for commercial speculators to make money out of lodging houses. It remained the case that little outlay was expended on furniture – other than beds – and keepers made significant sums by selling food to lodgers and charging them for minding their valuables.

Many owners and keepers were also adept at manipulating the poor law system to their advantage. They stood for election to the parish board of governors and even district boards and used their position to ensure that their customers received outdoor relief – which paid for their accommodation.

Approximately three-quarters of London's low lodging houses were managed by someone other than the owner and it seems that the rougher the establishment the more owners were anxious to distance themselves from the day-to-day running of the place. There were as many women as men keepers, but as to the character of such people, this varied with the nature of the establishment, from 'civil and decent' to 'roguish and insolent'.

Keepers were more notorious than owners. A successful keeper had to be a man of many parts. He certainly needed something of the entrepreneur, but his authority was often tested and could only be maintained if he was physically capable of ejecting the troublesome and keeping them out. He therefore needed a certain physical authority or, as one observer put it, 'had to have something of the bully about him'. He needed to balance the requirements of his clients, who often straddled the world of crime and that of honest labour, on the one hand, and, on the other, those of the police who expected a degree of co-operation. It was generally acknowledged that many nineteenth century keepers were ambivalent in their attitude to the law.

Most of the houses in the notorious Dorset Street district were owned by middle class entrepreneurs and investors, who did not live in the area but entrusted their running to wardens or keepers. Many of these people were 'known to the police' and had more than a fleeting familiarity with the criminal world. Because of the nature of the clients lodging houses attracted in poor areas, the wise owner generally employed both a keeper and what was usually known as a 'night-watchman' who doubled as a bouncer. The latter's role was to eject those who could not pay, which he did regardless of their condition. Hence the hopelessly drunk, the penniless and the sick, male and female, were likely to find themselves on the streets, regardless of the weather.

Detective Sergeant Leeson, who had an intimate knowledge of the streets around Commercial Road at the end of the nineteenth century, had a low opinion of managers, claiming that they were 'greater criminals than the unfortunate wretches who have to live under their roofs'.

Despite the many talents required to manage a house the wage was generally very low. In 1851 Mayhew estimated it at between 7s and 12s a week, which was roughly the wage of a farm labourer and significantly less than a London labourer earned. Keepers invariably got free family accommodation but still found it necessary to supplement their income. Many insisted that lodgers tip them on arrival.

Keepers frequently employed staff, usually to work in the kitchen and to clean. Invariably these people were recruited from the lodgers. They too supplemented their income by running errands for other lodgers. These were often people who fitted in nowhere else but found a niche serving those at the bottom of the social hierarchy. W.H. Davies had little regard for them, damning most of them as 'narks'. They often cut hair, patched clothes and mended boots. They sometimes washed the shirts of lodgers and there are several accounts of clothes being so verminous that it was necessary to first lay them out on the stone floor and assault them with a broom.

One of the most intriguing accounts of a manager is provided by James Greenwood in 1874 in his description of Pugmaster's Lodging House, Pugmaster Lane, between Bishopsgate and Whitechapel. The manager was a slim young man, his shirt dirty and his greasy trousers held in place by a leather belt. His face was as grimy as his hands and his long hair, lank and beautifully oiled.

His domain, long ago a splendid mansion, is a registered lodging house and he insists that the regulations requiring separation of the sexes are rigidly enforced and that anyone seeking to violate them is thrown out.

However, the requirement that each married couple should have a room to themselves was not adhered to nor were the ventilation requirements. Married couples were instead allocated a section of a room partitioned off by flimsy strips of half inch deal, for which they were charged 6d a night and more for children. In the men's room the air was redolent of rum and there was a man lying in bed during the day. The deputy referred to him as the 'bedridden'. An arm, a hand holding a bottle, a green nightcap and a pair of bloodshot eyes were all that was visible over the coverlet. It transpired that he was the establishment's best customer, having stayed in his bed for three months continuously, without once removing his trousers, sustaining himself solely on the drink the deputy fetched for him. In another room were a number of girls who made a living selling flowers.

Visiting another such house between Field Lane and the West End in 1865, Thomas Archer encountered a 'manager' or 'foreman' responsible for two lodging houses. He was a young man, wearing a white apron and 'giving the appearance of a barman at a respectable tavern'. The more interesting character, however, was the proprietor of the house that held between 80 and 100 people. This man's general appearance was that of a 'highly respectable vestryman in his year-before-last's suit of clothes, and with the confirmed habit of going to bed without taking them off'. Despite the apparent respectability of both men, police reports described both houses as 'thieves' kitchen'.

Writing of lodging houses in the Borough in the 1880s, Greenwood tells of the manner in which most keepers passed the night. The front doors of these houses were seldom closed and never locked and the traveller looking for a bed at dead of night had merely to push the door open, where he would generally find the deputy dozing beside his glowing brazier. He takes the money and issues the patron with a tin ticket. The lodger bundles up his clothes and puts them under the bolster for safe keeping, as it is taken for granted that anything left 'lying about' will be stolen.

Indeed, keepers were widely believed to be dishonest and were deemed no better than their worst customer, which is hardly surprising if, as Mayhew suggests, many had once been travellers themselves. Analysis of national data suggests that keepers knew their clients and had a great deal in common with them. Many had similar jobs and bought for recycling the materials which their lodgers gathered. Many were notorious fences, who dealt especially in stolen food which they often bought from their lodgers before selling it to others. Some kept children specifically for the purpose of stealing or begging, the proceeds of which they appropriated. When their lodgers could not pay for a bed, the keeper, it was said, sent them out to steal what they owed.

'Rapacious, mean and often dishonest,' as described by Mayhew, was by no means the worst that was said of them. The consensus was that they were 'men and women of the lowest grade whose ideas of morality are exceedingly plastic'. Like many others, Manchester's Head Constable held them entirely responsible for the conditions in which their lodgers lived and denounced them when he discovered 'in one room, totally destitute of furniture, three men and two women lying on the bare floor, without straw and with bricks only for their pillows'.

Keepers often claimed that they were the victims of their lodgers and it is certainly true that they had to take precautions against the compulsion of many of their guests to steal anything that was not immovable. The rugs used as bed covers were commonly stamped with STOP THIEF and utensils, pokers and furniture were chained up or fixed to the floor. Two Birmingham keepers who came to Chadwick's attention in 1842 went further still: they locked all their guests in the sleeping area, 'otherwise they would steal anything that was moveable'.

Many keepers were pro-active in filling their lodging houses. Those who owned drinking establishments, rather than directing their sodden patrons homeward with a cheery word of encouragement, steered them into one of their own beds. Others employed people to stand outside nearby pubs and round up likely clients, often enticing them with the promise of illicit drink.

One of Mayhew's informants, a veteran of lodging houses throughout Britain, told him that the most lawless and disorderly houses were those in London, though the most villainous keepers were to be found in rural areas. Other informants corroborated this view, asserting that even in low houses in the capital the master or keeper was generally not involved with stolen goods, whereas this was common in the country.

Lodging houses and crime were inextricably linked in the popular imagination. As early as 1839 a young criminal told a Parliamentary Commission that he was the helpless victim of the pernicious influence of the lodging house, for it was there that he was 'enticed into crime' and, he assured his audience, 'if a lad ever gets into a lodging house, it's all up with him'. No less an authority than Lord Shaftesbury fully agreed: 'it is there that nine-tenths of the great crimes, the burglaries, and murders, and violence that desolates society are conceived and hatched'. In 'kid kens' gangs of children were housed and fed in return for the proceeds of their crimes. The most infamous of these was run by Ikey Solomon, on whom Dickens based Fagin in *Oliver Twist*.

Mayhew concluded after interviewing 150 of the lowest class of male juvenile criminals that fences who ran or operated from lodging houses did in fact often use children, whom they fed and sent out to steal on their behalf. They often rewarded them with beer and tobacco. These fences came in all shapes and sizes. In particular they varied greatly in their commitment to criminal activity. At one extreme, the fence was the leader of a criminal gang, the 'putter-up', who planned and financed crimes while keeping a safe distance from the actual crime. A lodging house provided a means of maintaining criminal contacts without immediately attracting the attention of the police.

There were always petty criminals in the lodging houses who were prepared to act as intermediaries or fences on a small scale. They bought items of little value, often from children, and sold them to an established fence or disposed of them personally at a small profit.

The best fences, of course, were those who never came to the attention of the police and therefore left no record of their activities. These tended to be the ones who flourished and eventually operated on a large scale. They worked exclusively through dependable contacts, acting on behalf of novice crooks and all those outside the closed circle of trusted associates. This was, from the police's point of view, the worst of all possible worlds as it meant that stolen goods disappeared without trace. Far better that they pass through the hands of pawnbrokers who, though not scrupulously honest, might on occasion help the police.

There is no doubt that criminals were a constant presence in most lodging houses, and the repeated stories of unwary lodgers having their valuables and even their clothes and boots stolen suggest there was little honour among thieves and not much fellow feeling. Theft was a recurring cause of fights among lodgers and there is ample evidence to suggest that keepers were not always blameless. The landlord took no responsibility for inmates' belongings and the naive and trusting were likely to learn very quickly that 'a man must be very sharp to stay long without becoming the victim of petty theft'. This explains why many a wily lodger slept in his entire wardrobe, knowing that this made it less likely that he would wake in the morning to find he did not have a shirt for his back.

The problem of crime was larger in London than elsewhere and the Cockney wrong 'un was generally regarded as being of a different calibre from his provincial confrère. In terms of expertise in the black arts of skulduggery, he deferred to none: he was the master of his trade. With this came an intractable recalcitrance, which made him irredeemable, a recidivist of the most obdurate type.

In his letters to the *Chronicle* in 1848–9, Mayhew spoke of the criminals he found in a lodging house near London Docks. The pickpockets there were generally from the bottom end of their profession, specialising in handkerchiefs and whatever they could lift from stalls and shops, anything easily disposed of. In particular, there was always a ready market for food in the lodging house.

Housebreakers – near the top of the criminal hierarchy – were believed generally to live with prostitutes. Like many others, Mayhew found a number of small-scale fences of the sort that few lodging houses lacked. The culture of the lodging houses accepted stealing as the norm. Most of the thieves were young boys under the age of 21. Many occasionally resorted to work, but only for as long as necessary to meet their immediate needs and to enable them to indulge their liking for 'low prostitutes'. Burglars regarded themselves as superior to pickpockets and eschewed their company.

At the bottom of the hierarchy of theft were the beggars, many of whom specialised in cadging food from servants in respectable houses, which they then sold in the lodging house. Unsurprisingly, conversation in such houses tended to centre on the best ways to steal and the most propitious places for exercising the nefarious arts. The age structure of the occupants in the thieves' houses Mayhew visited fitted that found by other researchers: only 6 were over 40-years-old; 15 between 30 and 40-years-old; 16 between 20 and 30-years-old; and 18 between 10 and 20-years-old. Of these, 16 were born in London, 9 were Irish and, apart from 2 Germans and 2 Americans, the rest were from all over the country.

Most interesting perhaps was the information these lodgers gave about how long they had been out of regular employment and 'knocking about'. All but eight answered between two and ten years. Their earnings in the previous week averaged less than 5s. Of the fifty-five men present, thirty-four had been in prison at least once and one of them twenty times, with an average of four imprisonments each. Of the total number of 140 imprisonments, 63 were for vagrancy and 77 for theft, always for small sums. Drink did not seem to be a major problem for them, no doubt to some extent because they did not have the means. Of these men, thirty-four admitted to being thieves.

Mayhew explained their way of life as the result of their being 'naturally of an erratic and self-willed temperament, objecting to the restraints of home and incapable of the continuous application to any one occupation whatsoever. They are essentially the idle and the vagrant; and they generally attribute the commencement of their career to harsh government at home.' Police reports at the time suggested that there were over 200 such lodging houses in London, each housing thieves and pickpockets.

Much to his horror, Mayhew discovered that there was a level below even that of his fifty-five respondents. Such places charged only a penny a night. Their customers were the sweepings of criminal society – the lowest prostitutes, the most miserable and inept thieves and beggars and pitiable vagabonds, thirty of whom would huddle together on the floor of a small room, 'a mass of poverty, filth, vice and crime – an assemblage of all that is physically loathsome and morally odious – a chaos of want, intemperance, ignorance, disease, villainy and shamelessness, that can be paralleled in no other part of the globe'.

Many of the keepers of such places were fences and all were indulgent towards the criminality of which their lodging houses were the focus. Yet, even these were not at the very base of the social hierarchy. There were some for whom even a penny was beyond their means. These were the people who would sleep under the railway arches. It is interesting that even they did not consider the workhouse as a possible alternative.

Liverpool's juvenile thieves had a reputation equally as bad as London's, while the areas of the city they inhabited were as wretched as anything in the capital. The worst area was to the south of Scotland Road – Byrom Street, Lime Street, Renshaw Street, Berry Street and Great George Street. In 1858 the nearby criminal district between Duke Street and Whitechapel was demolished, with the result that most of its inhabitants debunked to the areas around Scotland Road and around Ben Johnson Street off Scotland Place. Other infamous areas were those that surrounded Ford and Maguire Streets and the Vauxhall district around Chisenhale Street. Liverpool had a larger population in transit than perhaps anywhere else in the country.

Professional thieves from all parts of the country liked to keep on the move. For instance, Mancunians frequently operated in Liverpool and vice-versa. Thieves who specialised in stealing lead – a readily saleable commodity – from new buildings moved from one major building project to another. But it was not only criminals who kept moving. When the Tredegar local authority announced an extensive public works scheme men arrived from all over the country – so many in fact that the local authority made a contract with local lodging houses to take an average of 500 tramps every night.

Many of these were 'ticket of leave' men, released early from penal servitude. According to Manchester's Chief Constable, Palin, the city was a magnet for these criminals who were responsible for a great deal of local crime, drawn by the number of disreputable lodging houses. All the commentators agreed: 'low lodging houses', as the newspapers liked to call them, or 'flash houses' as the public called them, generated crime. This, as much as the unhealthy nature of the accommodation, was a major reason why they became the focus of official concern and regulation.

Chapter Ten

'Whitewashed, Cleansed and Purified': Regulation and Decline

Dishevelled men clustered on the pavement blinking and rubbing their eyes like subterranean creatures shocked by the light. Inside the house the commands of peelers echoed round the rooms, as windows were thrown open and the pleas of outrage escaped onto the streets. Two peelers drove the ragged men out the front door and the sound of heavy boots clattered on the bare boards above.

'Out! All out!' the peeler ordered. The clatter of metal bedsteads hitting the bare floorboards and shrieks of protest filled the house as the exodus continued. The pavement filled and overflowed into the road: women and ragged children, navvies and beggars, farm labourers and a joiner, his bow saw slung across his back and his tool bag at his feet.

A hefty peeler then banged the door shut, unrolling a notice from under his cape and tacked it to the door with his broad thumb.

'What does it say?' someone called. 'What's happenin'?'

An old man squinted from the pavement, his moist eyes flickering under gnarled eyebrows.

'They've closed it down,' said the old man. 'It's shut, by law.'

The events that took place in Macclesfield in 1851 were replicated all over the country. It seemed that the lodging house had been done away with in an instant.

In describing common lodging houses as 'nests of disease and misery of every kind' the Parliamentary Commissioners of 1845 were merely reiterating what had been the middle class view for half a century, when calls for regulation began. The London Constabulary Report a few years later confirmed the conventional wisdom that lodging houses were 'low and vicious' schools of crime. Regulation, therefore, was designed to control both the physical and the moral condition of the mobile poor particularly in the cities.

It is wrong, however, to think that prior to the 1851 legislation lodging houses were subject to no statutory controls. Police already had the power to arrest lodgers who had committed crimes and often used this as a pretext for entering houses. In addition, in 1849 several boards of health compelled some of the worst lodging houses to whitewash the walls and ceilings and to use limewash in other parts. In some areas, such as Chester, in 1847, the city improvement committee required a number of lodging houses to dig drains for their premises. These houses were later inspected under the Nuisance Removal and Disease Prevention Act of 1848, which gave local authorities the power to demand that lodging houses be properly cleaned.

Ashley Cooper – Lord Shaftesbury, philanthropist, politician and social reformer – was the moving force behind the Common Lodging Houses Acts of 1851 and 1853, which required the owners to notify the authorities of outbreaks of disease and put the onus for maintaining, repairing and keeping the house clean on its keeper and not the owner. These Acts also empowered local authorities to prescribe basic sanitary requirements, enforce the segregation of the sexes and prevent overcrowding. Officials now had a right of access and keepers were required to limewash all walls and ceilings twice a year. Residents were also obliged to leave the premises between 10am and late afternoon so that the rooms could be aired. This meant that the sick and poor had to walk the streets. Mixed accommodation – often brothels – was abolished.

In the euphoria that followed the Act the police in many areas turned out the occupants of lodging houses, closing 150 in the Macclesfield area alone and dumping lodgers on the streets, overwhelming the poor law authorities and causing an enormous increase in the number of people sleeping rough. This draconian policy was immediately reversed.

In other places the official response was more measured. In Chester, for instance, the city council set up a permanent committee to implement the provisions of the Acts, particularly in relation to adequate washing and sanitary provisions. Chester was in advance of national legislation as it took action against overcrowding long before it became a 'nuisance' under the 1866 Sanitary Act and pursued keepers whose houses were overfull.

These Acts of the 1850s are generally dismissed as ineffective and there is no doubt that they had many limitations. Several of these limitations, however, were the result of factors beyond the scope of legislation. Foremost among these was police reluctance to visit the worst houses at night. Daytime inspections were a waste of time, as it was impossible to determine the extent of overcrowding when most of the lodgers were absent. Even if a room contained no more than the stipulated maximum number of beds, there was no way, other than by night-time inspections, of knowing how many slept in each bed. Once the keeper displayed the necessary signs stating the number of people allowed in any one room he generally had nothing to fear from inspectors.

The requirement to air the lodging house during the day was extremely unpopular with both keepers and lodgers. Opening the windows made the place cold, especially in winter when the only form of heating was the kitchen fire, and drove the lodgers out to haul their belongings through the chill streets. Further, neither Act contained a workable definition of a lodging house. Consequently many keepers evaded regulation by claiming that all lodgers were family members. Both Acts unwisely provided for the registration of keepers, but not the premises or their owners; if the keeper was debarred from running a house, then the owner simply employed someone else.

The onus for enforcement was in the hands of the local authority and depended entirely on its priorities and willingness to ensure that the measure did not remain a dead letter. In many instances inspection and enforcement were beyond the resources of the police and in the absence of a precise definition of the term 'lodging house', local watch committees were able to restrict their activities to what they considered a manageable number of establishments.

The Acts, however, had a number of unintentional consequences, one of which was to put additional pressure on those houses which had not been forced to close. Some raised their prices in order to meet the new regulations and consequently forced many of the poorer lodgers to seek shelter elsewhere, often in workhouse casual wards and refuges operated by charities, where the atmosphere was harsh with discipline and cold, improving air.

There is also some evidence that Macclesfield was not the only local authority to use its new powers to rid itself of undesirables. In Chesterfield, for instance, rigid enforcement of restrictions against overcrowding seems to have been used to force out known reprobates. As these examples demonstrate, the impact of the Acts largely depended on how the authorities chose to use them. Chester provides an interesting case.

By 1854 there were 261 lodging houses in Chester, all of which the authority deemed to be 'in a satisfactory state'. This happy situation, however, was achieved only after eighty-eight keepers had been summoned for infringements and half convicted. The council's policy was to refuse licences without the required privies and supply of fresh water. This relentless enforcement reduced the number of houses to a mere forty by 1869, several of which were owned and run by widows taking in a small number of lodgers out of financial need.

In London, however, the situation was more varied and complex. In 1853 there were 3,300 lodging houses under inspection with about 50,000 nightly lodgers. Yet, it is estimated that about two-thirds of London's lodging houses were unaffected because they operated outside the law: unregistered, tucked away in the entrails of rookeries, they were largely untroubled by the efforts of the authorities. Similarly, it is doubtful if the 1851 Act did much to improve the common lodging house in other big cities such as Manchester, where lodgers continued to sleep as many as six to a bed while others slept on the floor. In Angel Meadow and

Deansgate men, women and children still lodged in the same rooms and in the corridors. A survey of 1858 classified seventy per cent of lodging houses in the area as 'filthy' and half of them had neither toilets nor water.

The 1857 report by the police commissioners on the working of these Acts confirmed that while regulation had not transformed lodging houses it had brought about some improvements. Many reformers believed that the most effective way to improve the quality of lodging houses was for local authorities to build and run them. The powers to do so were conferred by the Labouring Classes Lodging Houses Act of 1851 which allowed local authorities to buy, lease or build their own lodging houses.

The Act contained no element of compulsion: local authorities were free to open lodging houses if they chose but had to meet all costs themselves. Unsurprisingly, few councils were willing to commit to an ongoing drain on local resources beyond their statutory obligations. The experience of the few towns that did use their powers under the Act confirmed the reservations of the more cautious, demonstrating that, though it was possible to make a miniscule profit by providing decent accommodation at low prices, this was insufficient repay the considerable outlay of capital investment.

Huddersfield chose to venture where most feared to tread and was the pioneer of the municipal lodging house. The Model Lodging House, in Chapel Hill, was constructed out of an old warehouse in 1854, when it was the only lodging house in England constructed and operated from local taxation. By November 1854 it housed 680 people. Its prices were above those of most common lodging houses, with single beds at 3d and 4½d and separate rooms for couples at 6d per night. All guests had access to a reading room, where they could read newspapers, hear temperance lectures and participate in religious services.

It is clear, however, that Chapel Hill was open to the criticisms directed against the London models and those houses built by philanthropists: it failed to cater for the same people who used commercial lodging houses and was merely providing a subsidy not for those in most need but for those who were relatively comfortable. Most of the 4½d lodgers were mill workers, in steady employment who were housed in what was known as the 'mechanics' house'. They enjoyed the privilege of a separate reading room where the newspapers to which they subscribed were available and their beds were made up with white coverlets. Management reports show that single men were exceptionally sober and respectable, though the same could not be said of the unmarried women. Birmingham and Dundee followed suit in providing municipal accommodation. Neither was ever short of customers.

Further legislation developed the regulation of lodging houses. The Public Health Act of 1866 gave the local authority power to prevent overcrowding and in Chester, for instance, it seems that this was rigidly enforced as many houses were inspected several times a week, with the result not only that the regulations were adhered to but also that many lodgers were deterred from using the houses. In other parts of the country, as John Hollingshead found in his research into the rookeries in the 1860s, these Acts 'were enforced, or not enforced, according to the energy and conscientiousness of the local inspector of nuisances.'

Despite this, the effect of regulation seems to have been to restrict the number of houses given over to criminality and to increase decent provision for the honest working man travelling in search of employment. In Chester in the 1870s inspection was often carried out by plain clothes police and seems to have kept the houses reasonably respectable.

In 1870 Thomas Archer ventured into Spitalfields, that 'great poverty-stricken district, bounded by Whitechapel and Mile End to Shoreditch and Bethnal Green'. He was encouraged by what he found and reported that the Acts had swept away the worst lodging houses which so recently 'made half London terrible'. About ten years later James Greenwood visited the lodging houses of Golden Lane, in the City, reputedly 'the very ugliest neighbourhood in all England'. Rich in scoundrels, the area annually yielded its crop of coiners and smashers and was the natural habitat of beggars and cadgers and 'the slummiest of slums'. There were at that time seven lodging houses in the Lane which nightly accommodated all who could fit in their 500 beds. He found much improvement following the introduction of the Acts.

The worst accommodation was still provided by many of the unlicensed premises, known as 'hot water houses', which were still much in demand and seemed to operate entirely without police interference. These were small houses found in such places as London's Little Cheapside, Cow Heel Alley, Reform Place and Hot Water Place. They had no beds but for a penny allowed customers to lie on the floor with about twenty other beggars and cadgers. Just prior to Greenwood's visit a child had died of scarlet fever in such a place.

By 1870 the population of lodging houses had fallen slightly since the onset of regulation and the police were confident that they had eliminated them as a source of epidemic diseases. The Public Health Act of 1875 transferred responsibility for lodging houses to the local Public Health Committee. The standard of housing generally had risen by this time because of greater stability of the population and employment, improved sanitary conditions and the increased number of houses available on the rental market.

Under the 1875 Act the local authority acquired the power to set and vary the number of lodgers accommodated in a lodging house and enforce the separation of the sexes. It was responsible for promoting cleanliness and proper ventilation, taking precautions to avoid lodgers contracting any infectious disease and acting to prevent the spread of any such disease should it appear. In addition it had an umbrella responsibility for ensuring lodging houses were well-ordered. In practice, this meant that keepers were compelled to display notices stating how many people were allowed to sleep in each room. Where two or more married couples occupied a single room, each bed had to be screened from the view of the other beds, usually by a timber partition.

The Act required every public health authority to appoint a medical officer and a sanitary inspector, to implement the laws on housing, water and hygiene. The hygiene regulations in effect meant that there had to be a separate water closet or privy for every twenty lodgers, a good water supply and adequate washing facilities, and no paper on inside walls. Windows were to be open for at least an hour in the morning and afternoon and beds were not to be shared by males over the age of ten. The beds were to be stripped and aired for an hour a day and were not to be slept in for eight hours after being vacated.

Both police reports and testimonies before the commission of 1884 on the Housing of the Working Classes suggest that the keepers of lodging houses were not only remarkably compliant to requests that they improve hygiene by cleaning, delousing, whitewashing and limiting numbers, but also did so without raising prices: they knew their clientele. Cynics explained this in terms of keepers' self-interest, claiming that they wanted to deflect attention from the nefarious activities that went on within their walls. The right the police now enjoyed to enter lodging houses, theoretically for the purposes of inspection, undoubtedly drove the experienced criminal to areas where the police were not likely to go or to houses peopled by their own kind.

Yet, there remained pockets within the cities that resisted improvement. As late as 1909 Mary Higgs maintained there were still plenty of unregistered houses where married couples slept in open rooms with a bucket in the middle of the floor the only sanitary arrangements.

Wider developments were also having an impact on lodging houses. The Artisans' and Labourers' Dwelling Act (Cross Act) of 1875 empowered local councils to buy up areas of slum dwellings to clear and develop them. In London this led directly to the obliteration of sixteen slum areas mainly in the East End, such as Stepney, Islington, Finsbury and Whitechapel, including Spitalfields. Among the notorious rookeries swept away none had as bad a reputation as the Flower and Dean Street area. In total about 23,000 of the city's poorest inhabitants were made homeless. In Birmingham slums were obliterated for the Corporation Street development. The expectation was that philanthropists intent on improving the living conditions of the poorest would buy the land and build affordable accommodation. In a few instances this happened but the new accommodation was generally beyond the means of those who had been evicted.

Owners of private homes sold up and moved out. In most cases, however, the owners of the condemned slums used their windfall to buy dwellings in adjacent areas and convert them into lodging houses. With less accommodation available, demand for their beds was greater than ever and profits undiminished.

These developments also opened the way for a new class of property owners, people very different from the established moneyed and property classes. These were people who had started out with nothing, often locals brought up in poverty or Famine Irish who arrived after 1848. Many of these began by leasing a house, furnishing the rooms cheaply and renting them out on a weekly basis. This arrangement avoided the regulations that applied to lodging houses, as beds were not let on a nightly basis. The commercial danger inherent in this was the large number of tenants who disappeared while owing rent – allowance for which the wise man built into his charges. Middle class liberals denounced these landlords, much as they denounce payday lenders today, as 'rapacious men who are often dishonest' but they met a real need.

It was only with the 1885 Housing of the Working Classes Act that the lodging house was defined as a 'separate house or cottage for the labouring classes whether containing one or several tenements'. By then there was clear evidence that improvement was having an effect even in the most unpromising districts.

Thomas Wright, describing the area around the port of London, said that the lodging houses there were no longer the 'fearsome and noisome dens' they once were and instead were usually 'the sweetest and cleanliest' houses in the area. He puts this down to regulation and the fact that they were subject to inspection at all hours of the day and night. However, this does not necessarily reflect on the personal hygiene of the inmates; though the keeper made available washing facilities, many of the inmates were unable to resist the 'luxury of dirt'.

By the 1880s many local authorities, including Oxford City Council, had in place a licensing system, which together with frequent inspection by sanitary officers seems to have brought about a general improvement.

In the words of a 1900 report the lodging houses of St Thomas' were 'beyond reproach' and deemed clean, well-kept and not overcrowded. There is no doubt that they were better than the majority of private houses in the same area. Their lodgers too elicited praise, as they 'caused no trouble'.

In 1894 the Metropolitan Police gleefully relinquished control of common lodging houses to the London County Council. They had always regarded such places as the criminal's natural habitat and the focus of their inspections was never the public health aspects but the register of inmates. This meant that owners' and keepers' primary concern had been to develop a working relationship with the police. The new regime came as a shock as public officials adopted an entirely different approach. They had the power to insist that all walls were limewashed twice a year; that shake-downs, bunks, hammocks and mattresses covered in oilskin were replaced by genuine beds with clean bedding; to close 'doubles' – mixed sex lodging houses – which were usually a front for brothels; and to inspect regularly. Inevitably the new inspection regime increased overheads and forced many keepers of small lodging houses to close while the profits of the rest plummeted.

There is no doubt regulation contributed to the decline of the lodging house. A range of other factors, however, combined to bring about its demise, perhaps the most important of which was a major in shift in lodgers' expectations. One of Mary Higgs' respondents, a working man who travelled in the course of his employment, told her that no common lodging house compared with the Huddersfield municipal, which he described as 'a palace'. Owners and keepers could resist middle class censure but they could not ignore the demands of their customers, who were increasingly influenced by the working class desire for respectability. The models in particular and improved housing generally encouraged the patrons of the lodging house, in the words of one disgruntled keeper, to 'demand nothing less than a palace'.

These heightened expectations threatened the very existence of the lodging house, whose economic viability depended on keeping overheads to an absolute minimum, which could be achieved only by providing minimal facilities and spending little on maintenance and repairs. Regulation, to the extent that it was enforced, squeezed profits. Increasing prices was not an option: the model lodging houses demonstrated that to turn even a modest operating profit necessitated a price regime which precluded traditional customers. Even this was insufficient to repay any capital investment and made a lodging house an unappealing investment.

Ultimately the traditional lodging house, offering little for little, withered as it became economically untenable. Wider economic developments were working towards its demise. The vast army of peddlers, hawkers and entertainers who circulated around the country and were the life blood of many lodging houses dwindled as the twentieth century approached. As the population soared, towns and cities continued to grow and incomes rose among skilled workers and the middle class, demand increased to such an extent that it could only be met by a multiplication of shops. The gaps in the range of goods shops supplied, which had provided scope for the itinerant trader, shrank and hawking became the occupation of last resort for those unable to get regular employment.

Industry too was changing and with it the demand for mobile labour declined. The development of Britain as the workshop of the world and the major exporter of manufactured goods during the middle decades of the nineteenth century meant that fewer skilled men found it necessary to tramp the country in search of work. Skilled labour became more and more factory based and factories increasingly clustered in towns and cities, which reduced the need for a workforce that was constantly on the move.

This is reflected in the changing composition of the clientele of the urban lodging house, which was becoming apparent by the beginning of the twentieth century. Transients were now in a minority, outnumbered nine to one by those who regarded the lodging house as their permanent or semi-permanent abode. As the twentieth century wore on lodging houses became more respectable, more orderly and more conducive to the working man of regular habits. Rural houses, however, generally proved more resistant to change, especially those which enjoyed a monopoly in areas where they offered the only available accommodation. The demand for mobile labour persisted in rural areas long after it had virtually died out in cities and towns.

No single nineteenth century event boosted the demand for cheap accommodation more than the Irish Potato Famine when, in the period from 1847 to 1851, over a million people left Ireland. However, it was not long before the Irish demonstrated their remarkable adaptability and became the most fully assimilated ethnic minority to wash up on these shores. They progressed economically and became no more dependent on the lodging house than the host community.

The cities that gave rise to the lodging house were also changing. Mayhew reported that towards the mid-nineteenth century the number of squalid lodging houses declined, as many of them were demolished to make way for major building projects. In Manchester the Deansgate demolition did away with many of the worst lodging houses. Simultaneously, there was an increase in accommodation which provided an alternative to the lodging house. It is true that few authorities availed themselves of the opportunity to build lodging houses, but the few that did offered a large number of beds. By 1865 Huddersfield's municipal lodging house had 2,870 beds at 3d a night. By 1900 Glasgow had 7 houses offering accommodation for 2,166 men and 248 women. In the 1890s the London County Council had 3 hostels, which by 1906 accommodated 1,875 men.

From 1888 the Salvation Army's Metropoles sprang up all over the country. Bleak and functional though they were, they nevertheless created more demanding expectations in terms of cleanliness and order which meant the worst doss houses no longer had the capacity to attract lodgers. The Metropoles in London included the Ark, the Harbour and the Lighthouse. Prices ranged from 2d to 6d a night and those who could not afford even that could earn their keep in one of the Army's labour factories. It did not take the Army long to establish itself as the foremost philanthropic provider of accommodation and by 1900 its hostels were subject to the same inspection as commercial lodging houses. Though clean they afforded none of the boisterous camaraderie and raucous banter of the lodging house kitchen and many lodgers disliked the emphasis on moral improvement and the officious demeanour of the officers.

Yet the facilities of the Metropole were excellent value for money and superior to anything available in commercial lodging houses. For 5d a night the lodger got a warm, clean bed, a locker for his valuables and for an extra 2d a substantial meal, usually stew, universally known as 'Alleluia Stew'. Cleaning and airing took place from 10am to 1pm when the men had to leave. For those who felt that 5d was a little extravagant the Army made available until 1906 coffin beds at 2d a night. For the same price you could get a bunk in the women's lodging house, for 4d a bed with sheets and for 6d a cubicle. The Evangelical wing of the Anglican Church also provided lodgings for the needy but on a much smaller scale.

The expansion of philanthropic establishments, such as Rowton Houses, has been touched on. These were much superior to the typical commercial lodging house and accurately described as respectable 'working men's hotels'. By 1905 there were five in London and they immediately became the standard by which all similar provision was measured. Technically they were not lodging houses as they offered meals and were therefore theoretically hotels. They undoubtedly spurred on many local authorities to provide comparable accommodation.

The number of temperance and railway hotels also increased. The former in particular offered travellers excellent accommodation at reasonable prices. Joseph Livesey opened the first temperance hotel in 1833 and by the end of the nineteenth century they extended throughout the country: there were eight in Halifax alone and they were found in many country towns such as Banbury, Shrewsbury, Northampton, Oswestry, Oxford, Peterborough, Stamford and Wantage. As working men's clubs and commercial music halls increased, many of them provided accommodation for their entertainers and most railway companies built accommodation specifically for employees working away from home.

The mechanisation of agriculture, resulting in a fall in demand for labour and the increased building of labourers' cottages, reduced the reliance of farm workers on lodging houses. Fewer soldiers used them as the railway network developed and new barracks and soldiers' homes sprang up in the 1870s and 1880s.

The development of the workhouse also contributed to the decline of the lodging house. For much of the nineteenth century most poor law unions regarded casuals as an intolerable nuisance and did their utmost to discourage them. As late as 1863 the combined casual accommodation of all the London unions was less than a thousand. However, legislation in 1864 and 1865 led to improved provision by spreading the cost throughout the capital, with the result that by 1866 there were 2,000 beds available.

The economic downturn of 1867 increased the number of those travelling in search of work and led to a revival of the system whereby those genuinely looking for work, as opposed to beggars, were issued with way tickets. Distributed by the police or the workhouse, they guaranteed preferential treatment for the bearer when presented at a workhouse en route to a specified destination. The bearer was exempted from the labour task imposed on other casuals. Similarly, some casual wards issued 'bread tickets', which could be exchanged for food at police stations and food shops along a specified route. Where this system operated it made the casual ward much more attractive to the genuine working man in search of employment.

In addition, conditions in casual wards were gradually getting better. Between 1865 and 1905 vagrant wards improved significantly, particularly in London, where they became the best in the country. From 1892 those who managed to convince the tramp master that they were seeking paid employment might be released at dawn, thus enabling them to present themselves to prospective employers early in the morning. This general improvement, however, had at least one major drawback.

There is little doubt that the casual regime was becoming increasingly attractive to professional moochers. The figures confirm this: the number of poor law dependents remained constant from 1865 to 1910, while the number of casuals doubled to between 8,000 and 9,000 per night. Though these figures varied with the state of the economy, there is no doubt that there were a number of people who chose the wandering life, resisted all attempts to drive them into a more conventional existence and increasingly found in the casual wards acceptable accommodation.

The Vagrancy Committee concurred with this explanation for the increase in the number of casuals. Its 1906 report stated that habitual users of the casual wards – about 16,000 in London alone – were growing in number and attributed this to the improved accommodation. Each major city's casual wards had their 'regulars', tramps who made no pretence of searching for work and were regarded by the authorities as incorrigible. Their numbers were particularly large in Birmingham and Manchester, in contrast to the situation in rural casual wards where only a tiny minority were professional scroungers and where navvies, seamen and craftsmen made up the great bulk of inmates. The tramp ward census of 1896–7 showed that almost one in four inmates claimed to be ex-soldiers, though only a fraction could prove it: hence the expression 'playing the old soldier'.

The inevitable result of this increase in the use of causal wards was a fall in the demand for lodging house accommodation. Lodging houses closed at such a rate that the shortage of accommodation was already a problem by the early years of the twentieth century. Mary Higgs told of men travelling in search of work recounting the great difficulty they had in finding accommodation, many maintaining that there were an increasing number of areas where it was simply not to be had. Some had to resort to the tramp ward and occasionally, finding that that full, were forced to sleep rough.

As Zachary Edwards found on his travels through Lancashire in the years immediately before the First World War, the squalid lodging house survived. The 'Penny Sit-Up' still thrived in Preston, where in a room 25ft by 18ft up to 60 men slept on the floor with nothing but a timber block as a head rest, with no heating and no washing facilities. Nevertheless, by the beginning of the twentieth century most surviving lodging houses provided accommodation at least as good as that enjoyed by the respectable working class and in many cases infinitely better.

Like all institutions that survive over a period of time the lodging house served several useful functions. Its reputation, however, was from the outset so bad that many commentators focused exclusively on its defects and were blind to the real needs that it served. Many of its deficiencies were common to much working class housing and some were simply the result of the huge disparity between middle class expectations and the reality of the life of the poor.

Yet, even the worst lodging houses served useful social and economic functions. They were vital to the mobility of labour, enabling workers to travel to find work and provide services. The peddlers and hawkers, habitués of the lodging house, provided a valuable service to people living in the countryside who, in the absence of shops, were often dependent on them for basic goods. They provided semi-permanent accommodation for many agricultural labourers, immigrants, the elderly, the bereaved, discharged soldiers and the unmarried.

The political elite's preoccupation with lodging houses became something of an obsession with those who supported social reform. Inevitably this drew the attention of the political class to the wider problem of working class housing and public health. This in its turn fostered interest in the world of the inner city poor.

Without the lodging house the Victorian streets would have been a great deal duller. The travelling entertainer alleviated the gloom of drab industrial towns and narcoleptic villages where anything that relieved the monotony of relentless labour was welcome. Many of these performers were disreputable, in the manner of a favourite uncle, and others were rogues; but they bestowed on millions of people, especially children, moments of wonder and delight.

Though greatly diminished in numbers, lodging houses survived throughout the first part of the twentieth century. Near Covent Garden and other markets throughout the country porters still depended on them; in St Giles's theatreland, the sandwich-board men and those who made a living hailing cabs for the swells had no other accommodation and in Stepney and Bermondsey, dockers and sailors between ships rested their heads.

Despite what many commentators had their readers believe, all lodging houses were not the same and there was a clear social stratification between them. At the bottom end many lodgers drifted between the lodging house and the workhouse. Most lodgers were not beggars but were productive: once settled in employment they married and then rented. In the meantime, the houses played a vital role in enabling newcomers to adjust to the social and economic demands of the city and town.

The common lodging house also catered for the needs of a largely forgotten section of the population, what Mary Higgs eloquently referred to as the 'residuum'. It provided shelter, companionship and sustenance for those who would not or could not find it elsewhere. It provided vital income for many people, especially women, whose modest capital was their only resource. For those at the bottom of the economic pile, in the days before the welfare state, it enabled them to cling to the independence and self-respect that they lost when entering the workhouse. It even provided a place for those who would sleep among the pots and pans.

Bibliography and Sources

Books and Articles

Acton, W., *Prostitution Considered in its Moral, Social and Sanitary Aspects* (J. Churchill, 1870)

Adams, C., *Ordinary Lives a Hundred Years Ago* (Virago, 1982)

Archer, T., *The Terrible Sights of London* (1870; repr. Dodo Press, 2009)

——, *The Pauper, the Thief and the Convict* (1865; repr. Dodo Press, 2009)

Arnold, C., *City of Sin: London and its Vices* (Simon and Schuster, 2010)

Aspin, Chris (ed.), *Manchester and the Textile Districts in 1849 by Angus Bethune Reach* (Helmshore Local History Society, 1972)

Barret-Ducrocq, F., *Love in the Time of Victoria: Sexuality and Desire among Working-Class Men and Women in Nineteenth Century London* (Penguin, 1991)

Beames, T., *The Rookeries of London* (T. Bosworth, 1852)

Booth, C., *Life and Labour of the People of London* (Forgotten Books, 1899)

Burton, E., *The Early Victorians at Home* (Longman, 1972)

Dare, J., 'Reports', in *Working Class Life in Victorian Leicester*, ed. Barry Haynes (Leicestershire Museums, Arts & Records Service, 1991)

Edwards, Reverend George Zachariah, *Vicar As Vagrant* (1910)

Gauldie, E., *Cruel Habitations: a History of Working Class Housing, 1780–1918* (Allen and Unwin, 1974)

Gavin, H., *Sanitary Ramblings: Being Sketches and Illustrations of Bethnal Green* (J. Churchill, 1848)

Glazier, M., 'Common Lodging Houses in Chester, 1841–1871', in *Victorian Chester*, ed. R. Swift (Liverpool University Press, 1996)

Greenwood, J., *Mysteries of Modern London* (1883, repr. Dodo, 2009)

——, *Toilers in London* (1883, repr. Dodo, 2009)

——, *In Strange Company* (Henry S. King & Co.,1874)

——, *The Seven Curses of London* (Basil Blackwell, 1867)

Hammond, J.L and B., *The Village Labourer* (Nonsuch Publishing, 2005)

Haynes, B., 'Working Class Respectability in Leicester c 1845–1880', *Transactions of the Leicestershire Archaeological & Historical Society*, Vol. 65 (1991), pp. 55–70

——, 'Working Class Perceptions: Aspects of the Experience of Working-Class Life Victorian Leicester', *Transactions of the Leicestershire Archaeological & Historical Society*, Vol. 63 (1989), pp. 71–84

Higgs, M., *Where Shall She Live?* (P.S. King & Son, 1910)

——, *Three Nights in a Women's Lodging-House* (P.S. King & Son, 1905)

Hollingshead, J., *Ragged London* (Smith, Elder & Co., 1861)

Hollyer, B., *Coster Girls and Mudlarks* (Scholastic, 2006)

Jones, G.S., *Outcast London* (Peregrine, 1971)

Joseph, H.S., *Memoirs of Convicted Criminals* (London 1853)

Kay, A., *The Foundation of Female Entrepreneurship* (Routledge, 2009)

——, 'A Little Enterprise of her Own: Lodging House Keeping and the Accommodation Business in 19th Century London', *London Journal*, Vol. 28, No. 2 (November 2003), pp. 41–53

Kay, Dr James, 'The Moral and Physical Condition of the Working Class Employed in the Cotton Manufacture in Manchester' (Ridgway, 1832)

Keating, P., *Into Unknown England* (Fontana, 1981)

Levy, M., *Doctor Barnardo: Champion of Victorian Children* (Amberley, 2013)

London, J., *The People of the Abyss* (1902; repr. CreateSpace Independent Publishing Platform, 2013)

Mayhew, H., *London Labour and the London Poor*, Vol. 1 (Dover, 1861)

Mayhew, H., 'Letters to the *Morning Chronicle*' (1849–50, British Library, LD16)

Murray, J.F., 'The Physiology of London Life', in *Bentley's Miscellany*, Richard Bentley (1844)

Nixon, G., 'An East End Lodging House in the 1880s', *Ripperologist*, No. 22, 1999

O'Donnell, W., *Ins and Outs of London* (Lamb, 1959)

Page, S.F., 'Lodging and Poverty in Late Victorian Leicester: a Socio-Geographic Perspective', *Proceedings of the Leicestershire Architectural and Historical Society*, Vol. 68 (1994), p. 121–35

——, 'Pauperism and the Leicester Workhouse in 1881', *Proceedings of the Leicestershire Architectural and Historical Society*, Vol. 63 (1989), pp. 85–95

——, 'Late Victorian Pauperism and the Poor Law in Leicester', *Proceedings of the Leicestershire Architectural and Historical Society*, Vol. 60 (1986), pp. 48–62

Picard, L., *Victorian London: the Life of a City, 1840–1870* (Phoenix, 2006

Pictorial Handbook of London (1854)

Ritchie, J.E., *Days and Nights in London* (Tinsley Bros, 1880)

Rogers, H.B., 'The Suburban Growth of Victorian Manchester', *Journal of the Manchester Geographical Society*, Vol. LVIII (1961–2), pp. 2–12

Rose, L., *Rogues and Vagabonds: Vagrant Underlife in Britain, 1815–1985* (Routledge, Keegan Paul, 1988)

Rowe, R., *Life in the London Streets* (1881)

Rule, F., *The Worst Street in London* (Ian Allen, 2008)

Sala, G.A., *Gaslight and Daylight* (Chapman and Hall, 1859)

Seabrook, J., *Pauperland: Poverty and the Poor in Britain* (Hurst, 2013)
Simmons, J., 'Joseph Dare and the Leicester Domestic Mission', *Proceedings of the Leicestershire Architectural and Historical Society*, Vol. 46 (1970), pp. 65–80
Simms, G.R., *How the Poor Live* (Dodo Press, 2009)
Tobias, J.J., *Crime and Industrial Society in the Nineteenth Century* (Pelican, 1972)
Wise, S., *The Blackest Streets: Life and Death of a Victorian Slum*, (Vintage Books, 2009)
Wojtczak, H., *Female Lodging-House Keepers in Victorian Hastings* (English Social History, Hastings Press, 2002)
Woolley, L., 'Disreputable Housing in a Disreputable Parish: Common Lodging-Houses in St Thomas', Oxford, 1841–1901' (unpublished thesis for MSc, Kellogg College, Oxford University, 2009)
Wright, T., *The Pinch of Poverty* (Isbister & Co., 1892)

Talks

Hamlett, J., 'Lodgers and Lodging in Victorian and Edwardian London' (public talk for the London Metropolitan Archives, 25 September 2010)

Web Addresses and Articles

Common Lodging Houses and Surrey Towns – *www.exploringsurreyspast.org.uk/themes/subjects/living/9-2/*
Hamlett, J. and Preston, R., 'Spaces and Material Cultures in Charitable Lodging Houses in London, 1840–1914' (podcast via *http://backdoorbroadcasting.net/2010/09/jane-hamlett-rebecca-preston-spaces-and-material-cultures-in-charitable-lodging-houses-in-london-1840-1914/*)
Kay, A., 'Whitechapel's Angel Alley: Prostitutes and Property' (via *www.alisonkay.com/historicaljunky/?p=124*)
Mackenzie, Eneas, 'The present state of Newcastle: Streets within the walls', *Historical Account of Newcastle-upon-Tyne: Including the Borough of Gateshead* (1827, pp. 160–82, via URL: *www.british-history.ac.uk/report.aspx?compid=43337*)
Matthews-Jones, L., 'A Walking Tour or London's Forgotten Model Lodging Houses' (via *http://myblogs.informa.com/jvc/2012/07/09/a-walking-tour-of-london%E2%80%99s-forgotten-model-lodging-houses*)
Stanfield, A.W., 'Midnight Tour among the Common Lodging Houses in the Borough of Wakefield' (printed for private circulation 1870, available via *www.archive.org/stream/midnighttouramon132engl#page/n1/mode/2p*)
Victorian London: *www.victorianlondon.org*

Index